THE LAW STUDENT'S GUIDE TO DOING WELL AND BEING WELL

THE LAW STUDENT'S GUIDE TO

Doing Well

AND

Being Well

SHAILINI JANDIAL GEORGE

CAROLINA ACADEMIC PRESS
Durham, North Carolina

LIBRARY OF CONGRESS CATALOGING-IN-PUBLICATION DATA

Names: George, Shailini Jandial, author.
Title: The law student's guide to doing well and being well /
Shailini Jandial George.
Description: Durham, North Carolina : Carolina Academic Press, LLC, [2021]
Identifiers: LCCN 2021004206 (print) | LCCN 2021004207 (ebook) |
ISBN 9781531021559 (paperback) | ISBN 9781531021566 (ebook)
Subjects: LCSH: Law students--United States--Psychology. | Law--Study and
teaching--United States--Psychological aspects.
Classification: LCC KF287 .G46 2021 (print) | LCC KF287 (ebook) |
DDC 340.071/173--dc23
LC record available at https://lccn.loc.gov/2021004206
LC ebook record available at https://lccn.loc.gov/2021004207

Carolina Academic Press
700 Kent Street
Durham, North Carolina 27701
Telephone (919) 489-7486
Fax (919) 493-5668
www.cap-press.com

Printed in the United States of America

For my parents, whose love I miss deeply.
For my children, whose love sustains me.

Contents

CONTENTS

CONTENTS

Acknowledgments

Thank you to the administration of Suffolk University Law School for providing me the time and opportunity to work on this book.

Thanks to my colleagues in the Legal Practice Skills Program at Suffolk for their unwavering support and guidance. Each of you inspire and motivate me, and I am grateful to work with you.

Thank you to Carol at CAP for her support and friendship.

And a heartfelt thanks to the many students I have taught over the years whose effort, energy, enthusiasm, and friendship remind me each year why I love to teach.

Gifts from students, although they are the ones who inspire me.

Preface

(or, allow me to introduce myself)

'd like to tell you a little bit about why I am writing this book. I have been teaching legal writing at Suffolk University Law School for 17 years. You are probably either in such a class or have recently completed one, so you know how much work is involved, both for you and for me. My students tell me the class is challenging and that I have high expectations. I tell them that their employers will have high expectations and that my job is to prepare them.

To help understand how to maximize learning in law school, I research and write on the topics of learning, distraction, and mindfulness. This research revealed that not only do law students and lawyers face challenges to learning and focus, and a lack of knowledge about brain health, but they also face a growing wellness crisis. As I researched these topics, the deep connection between brain health and wellness became apparent and inspired this book. I mean "do well" in maximizing your brain's potential, and "be well" in the process.

Maybe I shouldn't tell you this before you read the book, but I am not writing on these topics because I am totally on top of all of this wellness stuff, a queen of focus, or perpetually in a state of

Zen. Rather, I have had significant personal upheaval over the last couple of years — big, life changing events. Not to get too personal, but my normally stable world crumbled. And then, of course, came the pandemic. To top things off, just as I was settling into my sabbatical to work on this book, I got hit by a car while riding my bike. The hits — literally — just kept coming. Through it all, people kept asking me — how was I handing all the stress in my life? I was so busy just getting through my days I didn't give it much thought. But now as I write this, I have come to realize that some of the healthy habits I cultivated over the years were my safety net and new social connections my support. I had already planned to spend my sabbatical writing on the topic of brain health and law student wellbeing. What I didn't realize is how much I relied on and needed these resources myself — both to help me focus and work with all I had to deal with — but also, for my own wellness. I hope that you, too, will find that building these habits will provide you a safety net and support as you navigate the demands of law school and then practice. That is, I hope this book will help you both do well and be well.

Introduction

*(or, your thoughts are worth
way more than a penny)*

Lawyers and law students use their brains to produce value. Clients rely on us to think, analyze, argue, persuade, creatively solve problems, and more. Literally, we are paid to think. But have you ever considered how to create the conditions for your brain to perform its best, for you to think deeply and clearly, to be in your best cognitive condition? If you were a violinist, you would ensure that your violin was properly maintained to create the best chance of excelling in your performance. Since your brain is your tool, so to speak, shouldn't you do what it takes to sharpen it? The same way musicians would tune their instruments, or chefs would sharpen their knives, you must sharpen your mind. Law students and lawyers also face a wellbeing crisis. Luckily, tools that promote brain health also promote overall physical and mental wellbeing. By maximizing your brain's potential and working on your wellness, you will not only care for yourself, but be better prepared to help your clients as well.

To help you in this process, this book discusses:

- How to cultivate the ability to deeply focus and deal with the challenges of the 24/7 digital age.
- How stress affects both brain and body.
- How increasing resilience helps deal with challenges and setbacks.
- Why we need exercise for mental, physical, and brain health.
- Why adequate sleep is important and how we can improve our sleep.
- How what we eat affects our brains and physical performance.

While I have separated the material into chapters, you will soon see that each of the core elements depend upon and reinforce each other. Each chapter ends with a self-reflection. I encourage you to take the time to do each reflection as that effort can help you take the material in this book and consciously begin implementing its suggestions into your life.

THE LAW STUDENT'S GUIDE TO DOING WELL AND BEING WELL

CHAPTER ONE

The Wellbeing Crisis

To be a good lawyer, one has to be a healthy lawyer.
Sadly, our profession is falling short when it comes to wellbeing.

REPORT OF THE ABA TASK FORCE
ON LAWYER WELLBEING

Please don't let all that I am about to say be too much of a downer. You are reading this book and contemplating your overall wellness, so you are already better off than the people you are about to read about. But generally, when it comes to wellbeing, it seems that law students and lawyers could use some help. Although most students enter law school relatively happy, by the end of first semester, stress, anxiety, and unhappiness are prevalent, and often continue throughout law school and into their legal careers. Various groups have studied this phenomenon, to particularly unencouraging results. For example, surveys show that 21 to 26% of lawyers have drinking problems, 28% suffer from depression, 19% struggle with anxiety, and 23% are impaired by stress. Law students fare little better — 17% are depressed, 14% suffer severe anxiety, 6% reported suicidal thoughts in the past year, and 22% engaged in binge drinking during the year.[1] Those are the surprising results of a 2016 study of 13,000 lawyers by the American Bar Association

3

Commission on Lawyer Assistance Programs and the Hazelden Betty Ford Foundation and a separate Survey of Law Student Wellbeing conducted that same year, which included 3,300 law students from 15 different law schools. The adverse effects on the legal profession — including the inability of its members to do their best work, fully comply with the Rules of Professional Conduct, or even enjoy some semblance of job satisfaction and happiness — is obvious. With the objective of doing something about that, the ABA, the National Organization of Bar Counsel, and the Association of Professional Responsibility Lawyers created the National Task Force on Lawyer Wellbeing (the Task Force). That group issued *The Path to Lawyer Wellbeing: Practical Recommendations for Positive Change (2017)[2] ("Task Force Report")*, which found, based on nationwide surveys of practicing lawyers, judges, and law students, that many are struggling with serious physical and mental health issues that are exacerbated, if not caused, by the way that law is practiced today. The authors noted that

> our profession is falling short when it comes to wellbeing. [Recent national studies] reveal that too many lawyers and law students experience chronic stress and high rates of depression and substance use. These findings are incompatible with a sustainable legal profession, and they raise troubling implications for many lawyers' basic competence. This research suggests that the current state of lawyers' health cannot support a profession dedicated to client service and dependent on the public trust.[3]

The Task Force Report's recommendations focus on five central themes:

> (1) identifying stakeholders and the role each of us can play in reducing the level of toxicity in our profession, (2) eliminating the stigma associated with help- seeking behaviors, (3) emphasizing that well-being is an indispensable part of a lawyer's duty of competence, (4) educating lawyers, judges, and law students on lawyer well-being issues, and (5) taking small, incremental

steps to change how law is practiced and how lawyers are regulated to instill greater well-being in the profession.[4]

While the vast majority of lawyers and law students do not have a mental health or substance use disorder, that does not mean they are thriving. According to the Task Force Report, many lawyers feel ambivalent about their work, and different segments of the profession vary in their levels of satisfaction and wellbeing. Many jurisdictions have commissioned their own studies, and the results identify similar issues. The relentless pace of work in the 24/7 age leaves little to no downtime and no opportunity to recharge. Challenge, change, and uncertainty are the new norm in today's legal profession. Some other reasons for stress, anxiety, and unhappiness include:

- **Pessimism.** An overall pessimism seems to detract from law student and lawyer wellbeing. Some theorize that the process of "thinking like a lawyer" is linked to the development of a pessimistic attitude. "[T]his process requires the closest scrutiny of spoken and written thought to identify any defect that may undermine an adversary's position or create future problems for one's client. Thinking like a lawyer is fundamentally negative; it is critical, pessimistic, and depersonalizing."[5] It can be hard to balance thinking like a lawyer (when required) at school or work but then leaving that skill at the office at the end of the day and engaging in other activities or skills to enhance your personal life and relationships.

- **Imposter syndrome.** Imposter syndrome is a term coined in 1978 by clinical psychologists Dr. Pauline R. Clance and Suzanne A. Imes referring to high-achieving individuals marked by an inability to internalize their accomplishments and a persistent fear of being exposed as a "fraud." Impostor syndrome is a "feeling of phoniness in people who believe that they are not intelligent, capable or creative despite evidence of high achievement."[6] It is generally accompanied and exacerbated by perfectionism and intense fear of rejection and failure. These thought patterns create a perfect storm of insecurity, anxiety, and stress. Women and minorities can be even more affected by this negative thinking. If you ever question whether you belong or are smart enough for law school, well, join the crowd. I think we all did or have at some time or another. A little later in this book I will share some of the challenges I faced in law school, when I often felt like everyone was "getting it" a lot better, or easier, than me. If that sounds familiar, you are definitely not alone.

- **The adversarial system.** Additionally, while attorneys can control their levels of preparation, their manner of presenting information, and their behavior toward adversaries, they cannot control the facts, the relevant law, a client's motives, or the behavior of judges, jurors, or opposing counsel. "American law has... migrated from being a practice in which [providing] counsel about justice and fairness was the primary goal to being a big business in which billable hours, take-no-prisoners victories, and the bottom line are now the principal ends."[7] For every winner there will be a loser, and even if something aside from winning or losing matters, it does not matter much. And pretty much no one enjoys being a loser, do they?

Appreciating these challenges leads to the recognition that we need to think about, and take care of, our wellbeing. What do I mean by wellbeing? Don't think too literally about this: wellbeing isn't defined just by the absence of illness but rather, it is a *positive* state of wellness. From a whole-health perspective, it can be viewed as a continuous process in which we work across multiple dimensions of wellness. Most experts divide overall wellness into six types of more specific wellness: emotional, social, spiritual, intellectual, environmental, and physical. If this sounds like a lot of moving parts, well, it is. But they add up to a larger and more powerful whole. Importantly, the way we function in one dimension can enhance or impede the way we function in another dimension.

The Task Force Report similarly identified six dimensions that make up wellbeing for lawyers, best represented in this graphic:[8]

Defining Lawyer Wellbeing

A continuous process in which lawyers strive for thriving in each dimension of their lives:

EMOTIONAL	Value emotions. Develop ability to identify and manage our emotions to support mental health, achieve goals, and inform decisions. Seek help for mental health when needed.
INTELLECTUAL	Engage in continuous learning. Pursue creative or intellectually challenging activities that foster ongoing development. Monitor cognitive wellness.
OCCUPATIONAL	Cultivate personal satisfaction, growth, and enrichment in work. Strive to maintain financial stability.
PHYSICAL	Strive for regular activity, good diet and nutrition, enough sleep, and recovery. Limit addictive substances. Seek help for physical health when needed.
SPIRITUAL	Develop a sense of meaningfulness and purpose in all aspects of life.
SOCIAL	Develop connections, a sense of belonging, and a reliable support network. Contribute to our groups and communities.

This book is intended to help you on this path to wellbeing. Each chapter touches upon some aspect of each of the dimensions. What will become apparent is the overlap between them. That is, it is difficult to be truly *well* in any one dimension without being well in *all* dimensions. Because so much of lawyering depends upon your cognitive abilities, we will start by discussing cognitive wellness, which is found under the Intellectual dimension above.

Stop and Reflect: How Well Are You?

Consider the six dimensions of lawyer wellbeing depicted in the Task Force Report and graphic above. Do you perceive yourself to be particularly strong or weak in any one or more dimensions?

- In which dimensions or aspects do believe you are thriving?

  Spiritual, Intellectual, occupational

- In which dimensions or aspects would you like to improve?

  Physical, Social, Emotional

Cognitive Wellness

(or, brain health: it's a no-brainer)

This is my new bike helmet. Because my head recently struck the pavement, but other than a slight concussion, was largely spared, the slogan "you only get one brain" really "struck" me. (You will allow me a little concussion humor, I'm sure.) Your brain is crucial to your success in law school and later as a practicing lawyer. Law students use their brains to learn the law and legal system, and later, to help clients. The concentration applied as a student is even more necessary as a lawyer, when clients will pay you to listen, think, research, analyze, argue, and persuade. In short, they rely on your ability to problem solve, to "use your brain," so to speak. Your attention is the commodity for which clients are paying. In that case, shouldn't you consider whether you are getting good performance out of your brain, given that "you only get one"? That is, shouldn't you consider your cognitive health?

What is cognitive health or wellness? "A healthy brain is one that can perform all the mental processes that are collectively known as cognition, including the ability to learn new things, intuition, judgment, language, and remembering."[9] This includes higher-order functions, like decision making, goal setting, planning, and judgment. Studies have identified six cornerstones to any effective brain-health program for improving cognitive health. These steps include challenging your brain, managing stress, engaging in regular exercise, eating a mostly plant-based diet, getting sufficient sleep, and nurturing social connections. These cornerstones intersect and overlap with the six dimensions of lawyer wellbeing and with the six types of wellness we talked about earlier. It is apparent that cognitive wellness is essential to successful lawyering, and also imperative to your overall wellbeing.

You may not have thought about this before. But even if you have, you may not have realized all of the factors that can affect your brain's performance. You may have been able to excel in high school and even college without giving too much thought to the learning process. But now that you have embarked on your legal career, and knowing that clients will be relying on your ability to think and analyze, it makes sense to consider how you can get the best performance from your brain. I am happy to report that much of what it takes to strengthen and care for your brain is also good for your overall physical and mental wellbeing. Thus, the dual focus of this book.

Stop and Reflect:
How's Your Brain?

- Have you ever considered your cognitive health? How? Or why not?

  Yes, b/c experienced brain fog, lack of focus, and poor motivation

- Consider the six cornerstones of brain health: challenging your brain, managing stress, engaging in regular exercise, eating a mostly plant-based diet, getting sufficient sleep, and nurturing social connections. How would you assess your cognitive health?

  Poor, only do Challenging my brain. Everything else is lacking

- Have you thought about the learning process and how you learn best? If so, how do you believe you learn best?

  Yes, learn best through examples. Visual learner

- What process has worked for you in the past? How well has that process translated to law school?

  Visual learning, translating well by making flow charts and graphs

CHAPTER TWO

Cultivating Focus in the 24/7 Digital Age

The true scarce commodity of the near future
will be human attention.

SATYA NADELLA, CEO, MICROSOFT

Are you ready for a story of how I had to walk to and from law school, uphill both ways in the snow? Okay, not really. But here are a few ways in which my law school experience differed from yours. I had no internet, email, texting, or social media. If I was distracted in class I doodled or daydreamed, and if I was distracted while studying, I probably chatted — I mean actually talked to people. In person. Face-to-face. My options for distraction were somewhat limited. I couldn't instantly be connected with family and friends around the country, or the world, while sitting in a quiet library. I couldn't buy a coat from Nordstrom while writing a book (that's just a hypothetical, of course. Or maybe not). Think about the very many ways you can be distracted. Have you ever considered whether all that information and distraction has any effect on your learning? Now that I ask, you probably know the answer. It's not necessarily helpful to be able to have a full (text) conversation with your mom during Contracts, or watch a football game on your phone at the library. But just how unhelpful is it? As it turns out, all that distraction detracts from your ability to pay attention. And that does not bode well for learning.

Part One: The Key to Learning

(or, may I have your attention, please?)

Pay attention, as I am about to tell you the secret to learning. Ready? It is attention. In fact, not to get too deep, many might say it is the key to happiness. Before we delve into why attention is so crucial to a happy life, let's think about why attention is so important to learning. But later in this book we will focus on why it is also key to physical and mental wellbeing, and therefore, to your success as a lawyer.

Arguably, human attention is the most valuable commodity there is. Increasingly, it is the ultimate scarce resource. Focus and concentration are shaping up to be the new superpowers that companies seek. In a society shaped by the constant use of technologies, our brains are losing the ability to concentrate on a single task for an extended period of time. The current culture of connectivity hurts our overall productivity and wellbeing. Yet we all fall victim to its seemingly irresistible call of shallow thought and action, which make us feel productive. We wonder what email or post we simply must see or what we might be missing while we simultaneously try to focus or concentrate on a deeper task. Shallow and deep thought are at odds with one another and we must recognize that and account for it if we hope to tap into the best parts of our minds to problem solve for our clients and ourselves. In short, we must learn to exercise the "muscle" of our attention.

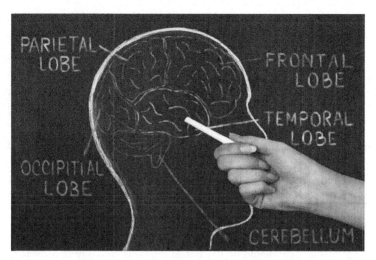

Parts of the brain (except yours isn't drawn in chalk)

But paying attention is not as simple as telling yourself to pay attention. Attention, concentration, and learning involve a somewhat complex process in the brain. The frontal lobe houses the prefrontal cortex, the brain's manager. This is the part of the brain we use for deep focus and concentration and where executive functioning takes place. Executive function is a set of mental skills that include working memory, flexible thinking, and self-control. We use these skills every day to learn, work, and manage daily life. Trouble with executive function can make it hard to focus, follow directions, and handle emotions, among other things. I think we can agree that good executive function is crucial to success in law school and as a lawyer. While you may not be familiar with the physiology of the brain, you might inherently recognize that deep thought takes place in the frontal lobe. Have you ever rubbed your forehead when you were deeply focused on a task? You were feeling your prefrontal cortex at work!

The sensory part of the brain is housed in the back of the brain, or the parietal lobe.[10] This is the part of the brain that constantly scans the environment and responds to stimuli. While thousands of years ago that scanning ensured our prehistoric ancestors' ability to respond to environmental dangers, or secure the food and water needed to live, in today's world the same part of the brain is ignited by emails, texts, and other stimuli. While this does not sound like a bad thing, when it comes to focus, it is. The more we use the part of the brain activated by distractions, the more we weaken the part of the brain needed for deep focus.[11] In effect, the frontal lobe and parietal lobe compete, and the more you indulge distraction, the less you engage the frontal lobe. Most of us find it hard to tune out distractions because our brain craves novelty, and today's fast-paced, social-media-laden, information-overload world provides it to us at a second's notice. (I wanted to say at a moment's notice, but frankly, we would be frustrated if it took us a whole minute to read a tweet, for example.) If left unchecked, we can easily live in a state of distracted hyper-connectedness, which feels good in the moment, but which diminishes our limited cognitive capacity and leaves us unable to deeply focus.

How do we learn? First, information is received through the parietal lobe in the back of the brain through our senses. If you pay attention to the information in some way, it makes its way through the working memory. Eventually information can become knowledge only when you engage the frontal cortex or the front of the brain. Have you ever been introduced to someone only to realize, moments or days later, you cannot recall their name? You were likely thinking about something else at the moment of introduction instead of the person's name. This happens to me a lot, so much so that I was very worried about learning my students' names when I began teaching. So I developed a routine to help me remember them. Before my first class, I spend time looking over my students' names and photos. During that first class, I have students introduce themselves and remind me of their names as I call on them. After class, repeatedly and periodically, I review the names and photos, and try to picture where each student sat in the classroom. You might consider this like the violinist practicing her instrument. I call on students by name every class thereafter, and am able to memorize their names within a week. My students are impressed and surprised when I tell them that I have typically been very bad at remembering names. I tell you this not (exclusively) so you'll admire me, but so you see the power of attention. I use this experience to discuss the importance of attention and focus in class. If I were thinking about what I might have for lunch, or glancing at a text message on my phone while a student was being introduced, I would not stand a chance at remembering their name. It is with concentrated focus and then repeated practice outside of class that I am able to do this. My students appreciate the effort and it is good for me because the very process of learning their names helps me practice the art of concentration, i.e., exercise my muscle of attention. But there are many challenges to our focus, so let's consider what they are and how we can handle them.

Challenges to Focus

(or, hold on, I just got a text...)

Now that you understand the basics of how the brain takes in information and translates it to knowledge, let's think about some of the challenges we all face in learning. Have you ever sat down to work, but found your thoughts going in many different directions? Or finished a study session but felt like you didn't really accomplish anything? Or stared at a book doing your "reading," but find that you can't remember anything you read? Conversely, have you had a time where you experienced razor sharp focus and were able to create something of value, where a concept "clicked," or you were able to write particularly productively? Researchers call that mental state a state of "flow," which is when "a person's body or mind is stretched to it limits in a voluntary effort to accomplish something difficult or worthwhile."[12] Some people call this being in the "zone" or "on a roll."

Whatever you call it, you know the feeling; during this kind of focused time, you get stuff done! Other times, you may sit in front of your books or computer, intending to work, but essentially just push papers, materials, or thoughts around but not really accomplish anything. What constitutes the difference between these two work states, and how do you create the conditions for that flow? Cal Newport, an associate professor of computer science at Georgetown University and a writer who focuses on the impact of technology on society, uses this equation to describe the process of working in a focused manner:[13]

High-quality work produced = (time spent) x (intensity of focus)

Notice that high-quality work is not produced simply by spending tremendous amounts of time on it. Rather, producing high-quality work requires both time *and* intensity of focus.

You probably know people who seem to get high-quality work done quickly, and people who spend a lot of time getting that same work done. What is the difference between them?

Inherent intelligence? Probably not. Among law students, an intelligent subset of people, for example, the difference is likely in the intensity of focus given to the work. Put another way, it may be about how well one can pay attention to the task.

So, if you know that deep focus will help you create high-quality work, why can't you say to yourself: "now I will deeply focus," and then just do it? The reason that attention and concentration may be the most important commodities in the twenty-first-century workplace is because our lives are littered with easy and quick distractions with which we quickly become addicted. Between our phones, social media, the twenty-four-hour news cycle and other countless distractions which cause the average person's mind to wander about 47% of the time,[14] it's a wonder we find any time to concentrate at all!

Before we discuss how to develop that intensity of focus, let's discuss other barriers to focus.

- **Cognitive capacity and overload.** First, it is important to understand that your ability to focus is not unlimited; that is, you have a finite amount of willpower and focus and so you must make conscious choices about how to use it. That is your cognitive capacity, or the total amount of information the brain is capable of retaining at any particular moment. Your cognitive capacity gets overloaded when you try to retain too much information at one time, or are bombarded with more information than your brain can handle at a given time. Once you hit that point, your brain simply cannot take in new information and your efforts at studying will produce diminishing returns. This is one of the reasons long cramming sessions are ineffective for deep learning.

- **Distraction.** Indulging distractions like checking emails, reading text messages, or other "shallow work" requires less willpower. Our brain craves the novelty, FOMO (fear of missing out) can be a big pull, and technology makes it all too easy to give in. Since overstimulation of the parietal lobe causes weakening in the frontal lobe, the more we attend to and allow distractions, the less we will build and engage the prefrontal cortex. Think of this in terms of your smartphone: if your WiFi and/or Bluetooth are constantly scanning the environment for connections, your phone's battery can get depleted. That is what distraction can do to your brain's ability to learn: it drains the resources needed to engage in deep focus.

- **Multitasking.** Another challenge to focus is our desire to multitask. Where you might think you are multitasking when you try to do multiple things at a time, like reading for class, checking email, chatting with a friend, checking a sports score, etc., in reality, what we do is more "task switching." There is an attention residue that switches with you, meaning that your mind may still be engaged in the prior task, especially if it is unfinished, and it takes a lot of mental energy to shift that focus. Each time you switch, you waste time and efficiency. Moreover, too much task switching can deplete that finite amount of willpower you have to focus. In fact, frequent switching trains your brain to constantly want novelty and weakens the mental muscle responsible for organizing the many sources vying for your attention.

> **Your Brain on Multitasking**
>
> The Institute of Psychiatry at King's College London compared the cognitive ability of people who had been multitasking with people who had just smoked marijuana. Who came out on top? The drug-affected workers. Why? Researchers found multitasking is incredibly stressful on the brain, impairs short-term memory and concentration, and essentially destroys focus. You probably wouldn't smoke marijuana while studying. Maybe you shouldn't multitask either.[15]

- **Procrastination.** Procrastination is also a barrier to focus. Our human nature wants to leave undesirable tasks for last — or leave them behind altogether, but oftentimes, doing those tasks first will yield the highest benefits and impact. Let's say you are behind in Property and know that you need to read a difficult case or work on a concept, or you need to work on your legal writing memo, but every time you try to work on it, you just get stuck. You avoid doing these tasks because they are hard and it feels like it will take too much effort. When you avoid them and work on other assignments, your brain may still be pondering the other undone work or engaged in worrying about how you need to do it. That is also detrimental to your focus.

In Part Two we will discuss concrete and specific ways to improve your focus.

Stop and Reflect: How Well Do You Focus?

Let's practice working in a focused manner. Set a timer for ten minutes, put your phone or other electronic devices in another room (really!), and complete the following questions.

Recall an unproductive study session:

- Where were you? _____
- What were you studying? _____
- How do you know it was unsuccessful? _____
- To what can you attribute that lack of success? _____
  _____

- Think about that session in terms of the equation: **high-quality work produced = (time spent) x (intensity of focus)** and determine why or how your study session may not have been successful.
  _____
  _____

- Did distraction, multitasking, or procrastination play any role in your studying? How? _____
  _____
  _____

Continued

Continued

Recall a successful study session:

- Where were you? _____
- What were you studying? _____
- How do you know it was successful? _____
- To what can you attribute that success? _____
  _____

- Think about that session in terms of the equation: **high-quality work produced = (time spent) x (intensity of focus)** and determine why or how your study session was successful. _____
  _____
  _____

How will you plan your study sessions in the future, given your observations now? _____
_____
_____

How might you change the way you study after reading this chapter and reflecting on your study sessions? _____
_____

Part Two: Tips to Help You Focus

*(or, hocus pocus, find your focus: no wand needed,
but you'll have to put your phone away)*

Hopefully, we can agree that distraction, multitasking, and procrastination are bad for focus. The good news is that focus is like a muscle that can be strengthened by exercising it, much like you can strengthen your other muscles. Here are some tips to help you exercise your brain muscles to focus better.

Distance distractions.

Distraction interferes with focus, both physiologically and mentally. And because we are so used to being distracted, these are hard habits to break. Don't worry, I am not suggesting that you disconnect from the modern world permanently, but I am suggesting you put yourself in the best position to engage your prefrontal cortex and deeply focus by creating blocks of time where you don't allow distractions.

I am going to start with the most difficult task, and I know it will make you uncomfortable. Put your phone away. Not just face down next to you, on silent, but in another room entirely. Really. I mean it. I challenge you: do it now. Research has proven that "even when people are successful at maintaining sustained attention — as when avoiding the temptation to check their phones — the mere presence of these devices reduces available cognitive capacity."[16] So by leaving your phone on your desk or near you, you will unintentionally create a drain on your ability to focus. Your mind will keep wandering, wondering if there is something you need to check, read, respond to...Not a great way to start, right?

> ### Lost Time
>
> Count how many times you look at your phone during the day to check social media or your email. Suppose each time you look at your phone, you spend approximately a minute, and another ten seconds in transition each time. Calculate the time spent in those phone checks during the day. Does the result surprise you? What could you accomplish with that time spent on another purpose, like a study session, a walk outside, or preparing a healthy meal?

Now, let's turn to your computer. Mute the volume and turn off any notifications. Push notifications sap your brain's ability to focus and do your best work. "I'll just ignore it," you think. Well, easier said than done. Whether or not you follow a notification, your train of thought will be interrupted by your noticing, processing, and determining whether to respond. If it feels radical to disconnect even for a few hours, remember that willpower is a limited resource. What often happens, according to experts, is that we respond to a notification, either because we crave social connection or have a fear of missing out, and we act on it. And that can lead us down a rabbit hole of distractions and further actions, such as responding to emails, posting comments, texting, etc., until we have used up time that was meant to accomplish our bigger study goals. Then, when our essential tasks are left unfinished, this creates more mental worry and dissatisfaction. This is why procrastination doesn't really accomplish anything except drain your brain's finite resources. Those essential tasks will keep playing in the background soundtrack of your mind.

You should also ban non-technological distractions. We all have many things competing for our attention. Try to work away from people, noises, or activities which may distract you from your work. Put away bills, books, papers, anything that can easily capture your attention when you look up from your work. Invest in good earphones if you have noisy neighbors or pets and know that when you sit down to work, work is your priority. If there are nagging errands or issues flitting through your brain, make a to-do list before you begin and then you know you will not forget them. Keep that list with you so you can add to it as things come to your mind.

Stick to a schedule.

Planning your work thoughtfully will help set you up for success. Finding focus cannot be a random thing, by setting a schedule and sticking to it, you will be more likely to create the conditions needed for deep focus and that "flow" state of concentration. Just like a regular schedule for going to the gym will produce the best results for your body, a regular work schedule can help to create the best outcome for your focus. Following routines and schedules doesn't require you to tap into willpower, resilience, or your intrinsic motivation to get your work started. That leaves more brainpower for the actual work.

By schedule I don't just mean a particular time when you will work, although that is certainly part of it. Remembering that willpower is finite and that focus is not unlimited, consider the time of day that is best for your work. For example, I am a morning person, and know that my best effort is usually produced in the morning. Once I am up, and have had my coffee, walked my dog, exercised, and meditated, I am ready to engage deeply in my work. This book, for example, was written almost exclusively between the hours of 10:00 a.m. and 1:00 p.m. on weekdays. That's my sweet spot. You may be the type of person who finds her flow state late at night and then sleeps late the next morning. To each their own in this regard. Just remember, you cannot deeply focus for hours at a time, or most of the hours in a day. Experts suggest we each have, at most, about four hours of total focus to use during a day. I don't mean you can only work for four hours a day, I mean four hours of deep focus work. So, plan to focus at the time that typically works best for you, to the extent you have control over this. (Neither you nor I may be able to avoid having class during our preferred focus time. Sometimes we just have to deal.)

Be consistent. Once you set your schedule, try to be consistent. Consistency is key to developing habits and therefore is key to developing the muscle of attention. After you identify a general time for focus, decide in advance where and for how long you will work. Choose a physical space to do this type of work and make this a place you *only* do focused work. Try not to work in the same place you eat, watch TV, or sleep, as this sends confusing signals to both your brain and your body. Again, you may not have total control over this, but do the best you can to create a space that signals to your mind "time to think!"

Have all your materials ready. When you do sit down to work, make sure to have the space and items needed to accomplish your goals. You don't want to interrupt your flow to get a book, paper, or other items you need. Remember that the stopping and starting of tasks will leak mental efficiency and will waste some of your precious time as your attention residue lingers. Clear your space of items not needed that may distract from your immediate purpose. Ban internet, TV, and other distractions from this work space. Don't bring your phone there — remember, it is best to keep it in another room. Before you begin work, set specific goals, like "read all the cases for Contracts, brief them, and incorporate concepts from the last class into my outline," rather than "do Contracts." Setting your intention directs your thoughts to a desired outcome.

After you create these beneficial conditions, think about what you need to support your work: things like coffee or food, and

> ### Mind over Matter
>
> If you ever doubt the power of intentions, think about things like the placebo effect, from sugar pills having the same effect as Prozac, to non-alcoholic beer leading to drunkenness to fake surgeries improving health—our beliefs defy logic. In fact, mind-over-matter feats have been documented by monks draped in cold wet sheets, who then used meditation to increase their body heat and dry the sheets. It's clear that our minds are very powerful![16]

schedule appropriate breaks. You should also schedule internet checks during a break. Research shows that 50 minutes is the amount of time most people can direct their attention to a task. Then, a short break to stretch, drink, take a quick walk, or otherwise give your brain a break is beneficial. Most of us find it very difficult to be away from our phones or email for an extended period of time, so putting your phone in another room and disabling notifications feels scary. Knowing that you will give yourself an internet break midway through a study session should prevent the anxiety of disengaging from those technologies from further distracting you. And, you will not be away from any messages for so long that it should be a problem. Try to approach this as taking a break from your focused study, rather than the focused study providing a break from your social media or internet obsessions. This is all part of training your brain to focus. Remember, though, don't *only* take internet breaks. Use your breaks to refuel, walk, stretch, exercise — there is a whole chapter on that to come.

There are a number of different methods of scheduling time to work productively. One you may have heard of is the Pomodoro Technique, which takes its name from a tomato-shaped timer, which the inventor of the technique happened to have on hand. The premise is simple — break down work into 25-minute intervals, known as *Pomodori*. A typical cycle features four Pomodori, separated by breaks. The first three breaks are just five minutes in length, while the fourth break is a whopping 15 minutes. But the time intervals are not the only elements that make this approach a success, it is the mindfulness as well. Recording the planning, tracking, progress of your work, and time spent is just as important as the timing itself. Take special care to note tasks and estimate anticipated effort, jotting down interruptions, and actions. Productivity trends can be observed and, in time, learned from. Here is a quick how-to:

A Pomodoro timer

1. Get a to-do list and a timer.

2. Set your timer for 25 minutes, and focus on a single task until the timer rings.

3. When your session ends, mark off one Pomodoro and record what you completed.

4. Enjoy a five-minute break.

5. After four Pomodori, take a longer, more restorative 15- to 30-minute break.

Whichever type of scheduling you use, it will help you take control of the work and keep you focused.

Your schedule should include an end time. At the end of the work time, stop thinking about school, homework, memos, or exams until the next morning. That means no more checking emails, rehashing study sessions, cramming a little more review in, or strategizing an upcoming challenge. If you need more time because of midterms or finals or a deadline, then extend your work day purposefully. But once that time is over, stop work completely. Give your brain true rest time. Why? While it may sound counterintuitive, downtime is as essential to focus as every other tip I have offered here. How many times have you had a brilliant idea in the shower, or solved a lingering problem on a walk or a run, or in some environment completely divorced from the problem you were trying to solve? Some of my best ideas have come to me during exercise. In fact, I pretty much came up with the idea for this book during one particularly productive run. That happens when we let our conscious brain relax and let our unconscious brain work.

There is scientific research to prove that the unconscious brain can be better at insight-based problem-solving than the conscious brain. In one experiment, 30 executives were hooked up to an EEG machine to establish baseline brainwave patterns as they tackled a problem-solving task.[18] The executives then did a one-day workshop where they learned circuit-breaking practices aimed at improving their ability to think clearly and access their imaginative insights. A key skill is switching off the "try harder" cycle, that is, that effort to just push through and keep on working toward a solution. The executives were trained to relax with an activity that occupied their brain in a different way. At least 15 minutes — or sometimes hours or a day or two — later, they would revisit the problem. After practicing the deep relaxation techniques for a month, once a day, they returned to the lab to have their brain activity measured again. The results showed a 33% increase in cognitive function across the group, and 63% more problem solutions were generated. Several executives said they also acquired valuable insights into how their brains functioned best. They reported that routinely after a break, and often a run, the problem came back solved. Some executives commented that they used to get breakthrough ideas at odd times, such as in the shower, but they did not know how to trigger them. Since completing the training, the executives reported some ability to influence when breakthroughs occur: they disengage from the problem and actively pursue downtime.

As cartoonist Tim Kreider blogged in the New York Times:

> Idleness is not just a vacation, an indulgence or a vice; it is as indispensable to the brain as Vitamin D is to the body, and deprived of it we suffer a mental affliction as disfiguring as rickets.

The space and quiet that idleness provides is a necessary condition for standing back from life and seeing it whole, for making unexpected connections and waiting for the wild summer lightning strikes of inspiration — it is, paradoxically, necessary to getting any work done.[19]

Put succinctly, providing your conscious brain time to rest enables your unconscious mind to take a shot at solving problems. Most of us won't quit unless we actually schedule that ending time, and without that actual end, we never signal the conscious brain to quit working. So, get that quitting time on the schedule, and stick to it!

> *Think of a time you knew an answer was "on the tip of your tongue" or in "the back of your mind." Have you ever thought: if I just stop thinking about it, the answer will come? Voila — the unconscious brain at work!*

Don't ban boredom.[20]

You might think we already covered this in the last two sections: you know to limit distractions and allow for downtime. But here I mean something different. Assume you are already following the first few tips, but you still find it difficult to focus for extended periods of time. You would not be alone in this struggle. Remember, it's not so simple as just telling yourself to focus or having the motivation to do it. Maintaining concentration and attention takes practice. As the author Cal Newport said in his book *Deep Work*:

> Efforts to deepen your focus will struggle if you don't simultaneously wean your mind from a dependence on distraction. Much in the same way that athletes must take care of their bodies outside of their training sessions, you'll struggle to achieve

the deepest levels of concentrations if you spend the rest of your time fleeing the slightest hint of boredom.[21]

Research shows that once your brain is used to on-demand distraction — e.g., you pull out your phone at every moment of possible boredom like waiting in line for coffee, for a friend, or for class to begin — that distraction becomes a powerful addiction that impacts your brain's ability to concentrate when you want it to. When you fill every idle second with scrolling on your phone, you are working at direct odds with attempts to develop your focus. When you do sit down to deeply focus, your never, ever bored mind will find it increasingly hard to ignore the call of distraction. So, what you do when you are not studying or working is as important to training your brain to focus as what you actually do when you study or work. Please just be bored once in a while. I promise, your brain will thank you.

Shocker: We Hate Boredom

To study how well people tolerate a lack of stimulation, in one study, scientists asked participants to sit alone in a room for up to 15 minutes, with no cell phone, no reading material, no music — nothing to entertain them, save their own rambling thoughts. Afterward, most subjects reported that they found it difficult to concentrate and that they did not enjoy it. The researchers asked the participants to do it again, only this time they gave volunteers the added option of occasionally giving themselves a mild electric jolt. Two-thirds of the men in the study — and one quarter of the women — chose to take advantage of the shock option at least once during their time out. A shocking result?[22]

Mind your mind.

Another way to work on the muscle of attention is through mindfulness. In Chapter Three we will discuss using mindfulness as a relaxation technique, but here, we use mindfulness as an exercise to improve the brain's ability to focus.

You might be quite familiar with the term "mindfulness" as it has received a lot of attention and various groups are regularly practicing mindfulness with positive results, including Silicon Valley entrepreneurs, Fortune 500 titans, Pentagon chiefs, and more. Apple co-founder Steve Jobs attributed his ability to concentrate and ignore distractions to his meditation practice.[23] Of course, and unfortunately, much of that concentration went into creating gadgets and software from which we need to disconnect. The irony is not lost on me.

The American Bar Association has been promoting mindfulness since 2007. Various bar associations around the country have sponsored events centered on mindfulness, and some law schools are including instruction on mindfulness in their curricula. In fact, in 2015 I wrote a law review article, *The Cure for the Distracted Mind: Why Law Schools Should Teach Mindfulness,*[24] in which I argued that all law schools should incorporate mindfulness into their curricula. Research has proven the many helpful aspects associated with its practice, such as: improving attention, working memory capacity, and academic achievement; reducing stress, anxiety, and negative emotions; enhancing creativity, empathy, compassion, and counseling skills; and improving immunity. A 2010 Harvard study revealed that most of us spend about 47% of our time thinking about things other than what we are doing.[25] That doesn't sound like we are being particularly mindful, does it?

Mindfulness might sound intimidating if it brings up mystical or religious connotations. It need not be — especially in the education setting. Although mindfulness is inspired by ancient practices of meditation, meditative practices such as mindfulness have taken off in many places and forms as we try to deal with the constant pressures of modern society. You may think of meditation as a hokey waste of time. Try to set those doubts and preconceived notions aside. If you stop to think about the kind of attention you will need to absorb the intense law school experience, a mindfulness practice can help.

Mind Full, or Mindful?

I love this visual and I think about it a lot as I walk my dog. It perfectly illustrates how many of us operate, with multiple competing thoughts jostling around our minds. I envy my dog at those times. I know her focus is singular: a squirrel, a scent, another dog approaching. We want to train our brains to engage in that kind of singular focus too. Not a squirrel so much as a brief, an exam, a concept, an argument. You get my point. To work on achieving that kind of focus, your goal is to be mindful, not to have your mind full!

What is mindfulness? It simply means becoming more aware of the present moment and less caught up in what happened earlier or what's to come. If distraction is one of the biggest problems of the times, then mindfulness is the most logical response. The simple goal is to give your attention fully to whatever you are doing. That is how you can work on your focus: train your brain to wholly engage in one thing at a time. How can you begin to be more mindful? Remember that the practice of doing nothing and being tuned into your mind can initially be frustrating, but will be well worth it as you settle into a regular practice.

Here are some mindfulness exercises you can try. Remember, you don't have to do all of them; there will likely be some trial and error in finding what works best for you.

Breathing meditation. This can be very simple but also very effective. Mindful breathing is a very basic yet powerful mindfulness meditation practice. The idea is to focus your attention on your breathing — to its natural rhythm and flow and the way it feels on each inhale and exhale. Focusing on the breath is particularly helpful because it serves as an anchor — something you can turn your attention to any time you feel stressed or carried away by negative emotions. Here are two that I use often. If I have difficulty sleeping or am nervous or tense about something, either of these two breathing exercises helps to calm my mind. The counting can help tether your mind to the breathing, blocking out distractions.

In-out breathing:

- Breathe in to the count of one and out to the count of two. Repeat continuously.

Boxed breathing:

- Breathe in to the count of four, hold to the count of four, breathe out to the count of four, hold to the count of four, and so on.

Thought meditation. You can also try thought meditation. While simply observing your thoughts and letting them go is an effective meditation technique, and can be practiced for long periods of time, it can be helpful to take things a step further and "label" your thoughts before you let them go. You can do this by saying the word to yourself, visualizing it written, or whatever feels comfortable to you. Simply label whether a thought is constructive or not. This is a very simple distinction that can cover virtually all thoughts. Just label them "useful" or "not useful," and let them go. Or, you can label your thoughts with greater depth by classifying them according to their function. Thoughts that can be labeled as "judgment," "planning," "fear," and "remembering," for example, may drift into your awareness. Label them and let them go.

You can also choose a thought to use as a mantra, one that you say over and over as you breathe. Mantras are a popular tool in meditation. They serve as an object of focus for the practitioner. You can also use objects like candles, a bowl of water, a picture, or meditation music. The idea is the same: give your mind something to focus on. When you have an object of focus, it becomes easier to steady the mind. Something as simple as "peace," or a phrase such as "inhale the future, exhale the past" can keep you focused during your mindfulness session. Simply say each word or phrase along with each breath, or focus on your candle, bowl, picture, or music. Remember, there really is no bad way to be mindful; it's all just practice.

Here is one of my favorite thought meditation exercises, called "Be Here Now." Try it anytime you feel your thoughts are scattered, or your mind is wandering while you try to study.

"Be Here Now" Exercise

This deceptively simple strategy is incredibly effective. When you notice your thoughts wandering astray, say to yourself **be here now** and gently bring your attention back to where you want it.

For example, you're working on your legal-writing memo and your attention strays to all the homework you have, to a date, to the fact that you're hungry. Say to yourself **be here now** and focus back on the memo and maintain your attention there as long as possible. When it wanders again, repeat **be here now** and gently bring your attention back. You may notice that your mind often wanders — as often as several times a minute. Each time just say **be here now** and refocus. Don't try to keep particular thoughts out of your mind. When you find your thoughts wandering, gently let go of that thought and with your "**be here now**," return to the present. You might do this hundreds of times a week, if you're normal. But you'll find that the period of time between your straying thoughts gets a little longer every few days. Be consistent, and you should begin to see and feel improvements.

Now, with these general ideas in mind, here is a suggested way to do a basic, seated mindfulness session. Use any mindfulness exercise that appeals to you.

Mindfulness Session

1. Sit on the floor or in a chair with your back straight and shoulders relaxed. I like to close my eyes, but that's your choice. Do what feels comfortable to you.

2. Breathe deeply and slowly, in through the nose and out through the mouth. Notice your breath, focusing on the sensation of air coming in and out of your body.

3. As thoughts come into your mind and distract you from your breathing, acknowledge them but try to move on. I like to think of those thoughts as balloons floating by, or trains that pass in a train station. You are not catching that balloon or train; rather, you merely observing it passing by.

4. Don't get upset with yourself for having distracting thoughts. Your job is just to notice that your mind wandered, then bring it back to your breath.

5. Start by doing this for 10 minutes a day. The more consistently you practice, the easier it should be to keep your attention where you want it.

In addition to breathing and thought meditations, which are seated meditations, you can also practice mindfulness through movement.

Mindful movement. Movement meditation is often used by people who sit for long periods. It helps to get the blood flowing, especially to the legs, and to alleviate feelings of sluggishness or stagnancy. Mindful walking or running is also a great way to improve blood circulation and raise energy levels if you're doing seated work for extended periods (this means you, law student, particularly during exams and bar prep-type study). You may already be familiar with the physical benefits of running or walking (and there is a whole chapter called Exercise yet to come). There are significant mental benefits as well, and many people feel that their best ideas or mindful moments happen during these activities. If you are not a runner, please do not suddenly try to run five miles! Start slow and build up. Runners often talk about running as a way to work through problems, escape negative thinking, or overcome personal demons. Believe it or not, that is backed by science: a study in *Medicine and Science in Sports and Exercise* indicated that even 30 minutes of time on a treadmill could instantly lift someone's mood.[26] And in literature, memoirs of using running as a barometer for self-growth abound.[27] You may wonder how to do a running meditation. Don't let the thought intimidate you. It just means that you focus your thoughts while running. If you aren't sure how to do it, I've included a sample running meditation in the Appendix.

Walking meditations are particularly helpful and can be done if you are not ready to tackle running, or in addition to running meditations. The technique has many possible benefits and may help you to feel more grounded, balanced, and serene. It also helps you develop a different awareness of your surroundings, body, and thoughts. Once you learn how to meditate while walking, you'll consciously notice the little details and your mind can find a quieter groove. Doing a walking meditation is also a good way of being mindful without making the time for a formal, seated practice. There is a sample walking meditation in the Appendix as well.

In conclusion, in addition to the exercises and techniques discussed here, there are countless mindfulness apps, websites, and resources you can consult. I've listed some of my favorite apps in the Additional Resources. If you try one and it doesn't suit you or you don't connect with the approach, try another! Mindfulness does not come easily, remember; you are fighting a battle of attention, and distraction wins easily. But the benefits are innumerable and well worth the effort.

Stop and Reflect:
What's on Your Mind?

Do a 10-minute breathing mindfulness session. Set your timer for 10 minutes (by now you know, your phone should be in another room) and follow the instructions for a seated meditation, using either one of the specific breathing exercises or your own.

When the time is over, immediately jot down thoughts which kept coming to you. Were you able to pinpoint lingering worries or issues? Sometimes we are so busy we don't realize or recognize the thoughts that are playing in the back of our minds. Identifying and listing them should help clear your mind. You know what you need to do, and listing them means you won't forget. Try doing this type of a session right before you study. The Appendix has a four-step mindful study process you may use to guide you.

_____

_____

_____

_____

_____

_____

_____

_____

_____

_____

_____

_____

_____

Part Three: Learning and Working Online

(or, no thanks, pants, I'm working from home today)

As a result of the coronavirus pandemic, much of our learning and working shifted to home. As I write this, most classes and work are virtual. And working from home is likely to continue even after the pandemic as companies see opportunities to change their way of working sustainably and reap the benefits over the medium to long term. Think of less office space, less commuting, fewer business trips, shorter breaks, and greater focus for employees.[28] On the other hand, there are disadvantages as the lines between work life and personal life are blurred. Research has shown that for many people, the work day has gotten about 50 minutes longer, and that may only increase as the blurred lines between work and non-work mean we are basically living at work.[29]

Research shows that people who are good at "time crafting" while working from home have higher job satisfaction. What is time crafting, you ask? And is this different from scheduling? Well, yes, it is. Time crafting means "being very deliberate about setting breaks, boundaries and rituals throughout the day to help ourselves transition from personal to work." Here are some general tips to help you do that. Much of this goes along with cultivating deep focus.

Create a "commute." Remember when you had a whole routine, like drink coffee, eat breakfast, take the train to school or work, such that upon entering the building, both mind and body knew you were there to learn or work? You didn't have to tell yourself it was time to work. Well, we've lost some of that with working at home. Try to create a pre-work routine which allows you to transition from personal time to work time. When I commuted to work to teach, I used to read on the train. It allowed me to stop thinking about groceries, laundry, shopping, packing lunches, and even lesson plans, and just clear my mind a bit before I would get to my desk to prepare for class. I try to recreate that by giving myself 15 minutes at my work desk to read news and generally gear up for the start of work before I actually begin. (It is possible that some online shopping is part of that routine. We all have our thing.) It's my non-travel "commuting."

Take breaks. Okay, we've covered this already. But it's important here for different reasons. Just like you might talk with classmates at the library about a concept you are struggling with or work on an assignment together, you need to allow yourself a break from the monotony of you and the laptop. Try to take a break where you might touch base with classmates or colleagues, not to talk about work specifically, but just for some check-in time. It might energize you and lead you to more productive time ahead.

Avoid multitasking. Here I don't just mean that multitasking generally is bad; I mean that you should have clear boundaries between work and non-work tasks occurring simultaneously. We all have probably read about people making serious errors in judgment resulting in things happening that were unintended, shall we say, for the work audience. You know what I mean: people think their video is off or their audio is muted, only to learn that they were overheard, or even worse, seen (I'm talking to you, Jeffrey Toobin,[30] and countless others) doing things that were not exactly (or even remotely) "work." Or people think they are chatting privately but do not realize the chat went to all 100 people on a call. We are unfocused when we multitask, and when the lines are blurred between work and non-work, that distraction can lead to mistakes with real consequences.

Set ground rules for those around you. Talk to family members or roommates about the hours you are working from home and the ground rules during those hours. Assume that anything that can interrupt you will interrupt you — like construction outside your window, a UPS delivery during class, or a dog barking during a study session. Try to avoid these kinds of incidents, but know that the pandemic and resulting shift to online work has led to greater understanding of the inevitability of interruptions. (Remember the BBC interview interrupted by children that went viral and promoted a lot of conversation and understanding around this issue? If you don't, watch it during one of your scheduled breaks.[31]) I'm a fan of the scribbled "Do Not Disturb!" sign taped to my door, but since my dog can't read, it doesn't solve everything.

Have an end-of-day routine. Similar to how you will cultivate a "commuting" transition to studying, try to create an end-of-the-day ritual to signal that study time is over. Jotting a to-do list for the next day will help clear your mind to transition to personal time. A walk around the block or a talk with a friend (on the phone, not video…more info on that ahead). Pick something that will help ease you out of your work day and allow your mind to calm from work thoughts.

Zoom Fatigue
(or, lights, camera…inaction)

In addition to most of our work shifting online, much of our social interaction is also virtual, such that you might be online all day for classes and then online with friends or family afterward to socialize. We have Zoom coffee hours, happy hours, graduations, birthdays, bridal showers, funerals, and even Zoom weddings. (I have a Zoom wedding this weekend and I am considering whether any of my athleisure outfits is appropriate.) When you finish a day, which includes any number of these things, you are left feeling completely exhausted. Researchers call this "Zoom fatigue": the tiredness, worry, or burnout associated with overusing virtual platforms of communication. Like other experiences associated with the coronavirus pandemic, Zoom fatigue is widely prevalent, intense, and completely new.[32] There are a number of theories as to what causes

Zoom fatigue, but there is certainly consensus that it is a real thing. Though it's known as "Zoom fatigue," it can just as easily take place on any video-conferencing platform, including Google Hangouts and Meet, Skype, Microsoft Teams, GoToMeeting, FaceTime, Blue-Jeans, Slack, Houseparty, and so on. There are a number of reasons why this happens.

Video requires more focus. Being on a video call requires more focus than a face-to-face chat. We have to focus more intently on conversations in order to absorb information. Video chats mean we need to work harder to process nonverbal cues like facial expressions, the tone and pitch of the voice, and body language; paying more attention to these consumes a lot of energy. Our minds are together when our bodies feel we're not. That dissonance, which causes people to have conflicting feelings, is exhausting. In addition, on video, the only way you can show that you're paying attention is to look at the camera, but you're not looking at the person speaking. How often would you sit a few feet away from your professor or classmates and stare at them? In person, you can glance down or look out a window and it doesn't seem odd. On video we are afraid that we will seem distracted so we try to maintain that gaze. It's incredibly draining.

Silence is another challenge. Silence creates a natural rhythm in a real-life conversation. However, when it happens in a video call, you become anxious about the technology. It also makes people uncomfortable. Further, if we are physically on camera, we are very aware of being watched. When you're on a video conference, you know everybody's looking at you; you're on stage, so there comes a social pressure and feeling like you need to perform. Being performative is nerve-wracking and more stressful. It's also very hard for people not to look at their own face if they can see it on screen, or not to be conscious of how they behave in front of the camera.

Distractions are easily indulged. Video calls also make it easier than ever to lose focus. Admit it: you've done it. Turned your video off to run to the kitchen, or "quickly" check email, text a friend, or respond to a family member, even though we had asked them not to bother us. (My son just came in to get something off the printer, then wanted to talk about what was for lunch. I'm sure you feel my pain.) Things which you may not have done if you were in the classroom, engaged with the professor and students, suddenly become okay in the at-home work environment. Just because you *can* doesn't mean you *should*.

The lines between aspects of our lives are blurred. To top it all off, aspects of our lives that used to be separate — work, friends, family — are all now happening in the same space and that can be difficult. We usually have multiple aspects to our lives — context-dependent social roles, relationships, activities and goals — and that variety is healthy. Imagine you go to a party, and at the same party you talk with your professors, chat with your colleagues, meet your parents, and go on a date. Isn't that strange? That's what we're doing now. Pre-Covid, most of our social roles happened in different places, but now the context has collapsed and our only space for interaction is a computer window. It's easy to see why we might be stressed.

So how can you handle this "Zoom fatigue" and prepare yourself to work productively and (at least semi) happily at home? Well, remember, there are perks to working from home: time and expense saved in commuting, more time with family, greater potential for flexibility in your schedule, just to name a few. Each of these can become a negative, however, if we don't follow some basic tips. Luckily, most of this advice pertains to protecting our cognitive health more generally as well.

Many of the tips I offered in the section on focus, like taking breaks and trying to separate work from non-work, apply here. Here are additional tips to help with online overload:

- **Try to get away from your video screen for real breaks.** Don't just switch one screen for another. If possible, aim for a day a week with no video calls, and where possible, use email or actual phone calls (!) to communicate. Remember, not every conversation requires a video call.

- **Hide the self view when you are in a class or meeting.** We tend to focus too much on looking at ourselves, making us hyper-aware of every wrinkle or expression or how it might be interpreted. Our brains grow fatigued more easily by this. If you don't need to see yourself, turn it off. You may be surprised at how much easier it is to focus on the material.

- **Use speaker view.** In speaker view, you can better see the person speaking, including facial expressions and other cues. This taxes your brain less than scanning other participants' faces and backgrounds unnecessarily. Of course, this is not always possible but it is something to keep in mind.

- **Try to avoid back-to-back calls.** Your brain needs a break from all that focus. Take a break to do something totally different. Ideally, stretch and breath some fresh air, even if it is only for a few minutes.

- **Use actual pencil or pen and paper to take notes.** There is a benefit to engaging various senses as you work from home. You may be familiar with the concept of learning styles, and perhaps you have a preferred one. These styles or modes include verbal (learning through written text), visual (learning through pictures, diagrams, models), oral (learning through talking out ideas), aural (learning through listening to lectures, discussions, or recordings), tactile (learning through touching and manipulating materials) and kinesthetic (learning through moving and doing). Cognitive psychologists suggest that it's not so much that we learn better using one of these modes, but that by using different modes we have a greater likelihood of preventing cognitive overload. By making use of different modes, rather than conveying all the material through one mode only, we can take in more information.[33] Having video calls all day is overtaxing visually and aurally. Taking actual pen to paper engages the tactile and kinesthetic modes of learning, and allows your brain to function better.

These are just a few tips. As we continue learning and working from home, we will continue to develop ways to manage Zoom fatigue. Just being aware that it is real will help you think about creating healthier working conditions. Your brain will thank you!

**Stop and Reflect:
Are You Zoomed Out?**

Take five minutes to answer the following questions.

Outside of school, where do you do most of your learning and studying?

_____

_____

Is that space conducive to concentration? Why or why not?

_____

_____

_____

_____

Have you experienced "Zoom fatigue"? How did you feel?

_____

_____

_____

_____

List ways you can improve your work-from-home routine.

_____

_____

_____

_____

_____

_____

CHAPTER THREE

Stress

Rule number one is, don't sweat the small stuff.
Rule number two is, it's all small stuff.

ROBERT ELIOT

won't sugar coat it. By now you know, either personally or anecdotally, that law school causes stress. In fact, 96% of law students experience significant levels of stress, compared to 70% of medical students and 43% of graduate students.[34] Depression, anxiety, and alcohol or drug-related abuse occurs at much higher rates among law students and lawyers than in the general population. At first, you might wonder if this is because people who are prone to stress and its effects are drawn to a career in law. That's not really the case, though. Researchers believe that law students' mental health is similar to that of other graduate students upon entering school, but law-school induced stress seems to lead them to higher rates of depression and overall demoralization.

What is so different about law school? You knew it would be hard. But law school may feel more competitive and adversarial than you imagined. Although you were probably quite successful in school previously, law school is likely different and harder, and it requires new techniques to study and learn. Mandatory grading curves can be unforgiving and demoralizing. If you are in a new city and new environment, you may not have the same support available to you to handle stress as well.

Further, as discussed in Chapter One, law school can make you feel like an imposter, or believe that other students are handling things more easily. Despite external evidence of their competence, those exhibiting imposter syndrome remain convinced that they are frauds and do not deserve the success they have achieved. Proof of success is dismissed as luck, timing, or a result of deceiving others into thinking they are more intelligent and competent than they believe themselves to be. Some studies suggest that impostor syndrome is particularly common among high-achieving women and minorities.[35]

All of these factors lead to high levels of law student stress. Maybe you think law school is temporary and you can stick it out. That's not a great plan because you will be facing even more stress as a lawyer.

I suspect it will not come as a surprise to you that too much stress is bad for you. The very many ways it is counterproductive may surprise you, however. We are all familiar with the concept that stress causes mental anxiety. In fact, stress also interferes with your brain's ability to concentrate and to learn. Stress is directly detrimental to brain health. Excess stress can wreak havoc on your body as well. From headaches and chest pain to muscle tension and upset stomachs, stress can affect your entire body. And, as anyone who has dealt with severe stress knows, sleep can become difficult, anxiety can build up, and irritability can surge.

We should recognize, however, that not all stress is bad. The good side of stress helps motivate you to prepare for a task (like a book-manuscript deadline, for example). The body's response to stress developed to handle life-threatening circumstances, for example, encountering a saber-toothed tiger in the hunter-gatherer era. In that type of situation, the sympathetic nervous system kicks into gear. The body ramps up its reactions and devotes all its energy to facing or avoiding the danger or enemy. You probably remember a time your heart raced when you were faced with stress. That happens as part of the body's stress response: your heart rate increases so that more oxygen can be pumped to your muscles, and blood is diverted there as well. The stress hormones adrenaline, epinephrine, norepinephrine, and cortisol are released. All these physiological changes are known as the "fight or flight" response and they allow a person to survive in the face of an extreme threat.

While there are, therefore, positive effects of stress, chronic or habitual stress can be harmful on multiple levels, both physically and mentally. In our modern era, the stresses we face are not lions and tigers and bears (oh my!), but homework, deadlines, and clients, etc. The body doesn't recognize the different sources of stress, but it produces the same responses. Some of these responses are particularly important for us to understand, like the effects of cortisol on learning.

Cortisol is released for hours after a stressful event, and that excess cortisol can impair cognitive performance. It damages the brain and blocks the formation of new connections in the hippocampus, which is critical to the learning process as it helps information transform from working memory into long-term memory. The hippocampus is located near the brain's emotional center, the amygdala. Stress fires up the amygdala, which releases cortisol, which in turn interferes with hippocampus function. The more cortisol released by the amygdala, the less you are able to focus by using the prefrontal cortex. So, in short, stress can prevent you from learning.

Stress negatively impacts us not just by impairing cognitive performance, but it also dampens thyroid function, decreases bone density, disrupts sleep, reduces muscle mass, elevates blood pressure, lowers immune function, slows wound healing, and can also lead to heart attacks, strokes, higher levels of LDL (bad cholesterol) and lower levels of HDL (good cholesterol), depression, and more. Scientists believe that psychological stress can induce disease by creating behaviors such as poor sleep, less exercise, poor eating choices, smoking, excess drinking, and by releasing hormones which negatively affect many organs and the immune system. If I told you that there was something you could do to improve your attention, perception, short-term memory, and learning, I'm pretty sure you would say, "sign me up." You can impact the negative loop of behaviors that severely impact cognitive functioning, as shown in the diagram below, by working to reduce the impact of stress.

The Stress-Brain Loop

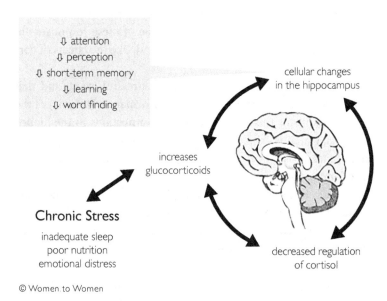

⇩ attention
⇩ perception
⇩ short-term memory
⇩ learning
⇩ word finding

cellular changes
in the hippocampus

increases
glucocorticoids

Chronic Stress

inadequate sleep
poor nutrition
emotional distress

decreased regulation
of cortisol

© Women to Women

Stop and Reflect: Assess Your Stress

Take five minutes to consider your own stress levels and habits before reading about ways to deal with stress.

1. How often do you feel stressed?

- Often
- Sometimes
- Never

2. How do you know you are stressed? Describe what happens.

Angry/ quick to anger, Back hurts, head hurts, Stomach hurts, racing heart

3. How do you typically handle stress?

Poorly... Usually talk w/ someone after I panic. Depends on the level of stress

4. List three things that are making you stressed right now.

Exams/School
Bar Exam
Driving in traffic w/ dumb ppl

Tips for Dealing with Stress

(or, why you can't just take a chill pill)

Okay, I assume we can all agree: too much stress is bad. And as we know, even if you were not a very stressed-out person before law school, the stresses of law school may bring it on as you tackle classes, mid-terms, memos, finals, internships, and so on. So, let's talk about how you can deal with it. Effective stress management helps you break the hold stress has on your life, so you can be happier, healthier, and more productive. The ultimate goal is a balanced life, with time for study, work, relationships, relaxation, and fun — and the resilience to hold up under pressure and meet challenges head on.[36] But stress management is not one-size-fits-all. That's why it's important to experiment and find out what works best for you. The following stress-management tips can help you do that. Remember, you may need to try different techniques until you find a combination that works for you, and even those may change over time as you encounter new challenges and develop new skills.

Manage your time. Creating a daily schedule may be one of the most significant steps you can take to reduce stress and increase your productivity. Remember in the last chapter we learned that creating and following a schedule for your work will lead to greater focus and productivity during that work period. But planning your day will also ease your stress in general. You'll be able to prioritize and arrange your to-do items and tackle the most important ones first, when you know you'll have the most energy. For most people (like me, as you already know) that's in the morning, but you do you. Most experts recommend planning your day the night before. Take the last half hour or so of your day and look over what you have the next day: assignments, classes, study sessions, meetings, appointments, etc. Map those out and make a to-do list of other things you hope to accomplish. Make sure to leave time for meals, exercise, and social connections. Factor in buffer and interruption time, and don't overschedule or plan. Plan more, stress less. That's your goal. Remember, though, that if you plan too much, you will likely stress more. It's a balance and will likely require trial and error. But try to avoid just letting the days happen; plan your days so that your days don't plan you. The Appendix includes sample daily and weekly journal entries to give you ideas of how to implement these suggestions.

Get enough sleep. We will talk at length about sleep in the next chapter. But generally, remember that operating in a sleep-deprived state puts you at a distinct disadvantage. You're less productive and you may find it more difficult to learn, and you may even be a hazard behind the wheel.[37] Don't neglect your sleep schedule. Aim to get at least eight hours a night and take power naps when you need them. I know this may sound challenging to you as a law student, stressed about midterms or finals or a memo deadline. Maybe you could pull all-nighters in college and figure you'll just keep doing that. But remember that lack of sleep plays into the stress-brain loop, and could

> ## Driving While Drowsy
>
> Driving while drowsy is dangerous because sleep deprivation can have similar effects on your body as drinking alcohol. Being awake for 18 hours straight makes you drive like you have a blood alcohol level of .05. If you've been awake for a full 24 hours and drive—say, after a night where you just couldn't fall asleep—it's like you have a blood alcohol level of .10.

end up making you more stressed, less productive, less able to concentrate and focus, and so on. You know that is not a good recipe for successful studying or lawyering.

Exercise regularly. We will also talk more about exercise in a subsequent chapter, but for now note that one of the healthiest ways to blow off steam is to get regular exercise. You may feel you don't have time to exercise, but you can work exercise into your schedule by doing yoga, walking or biking, going to the gym, and just generally being active. Take the stairs (free exercise equipment!), walk to get your coffee instead of driving, make plans to go for a walk with friends or classmates. How about a walking study session with your study group? Starting now and keeping a regular exercise practice can help you develop habits which will set you up to handle the stresses of law practice. On a personal note, I firmly believe that a regular exercise routine, which I clung to during these last few years as I faced significant stress in my personal life, kept me from becoming depressed and kept me going. Don't underestimate the power of endorphins!

Eat a well-balanced diet. Surprise: we will also talk about nutrition in a subsequent chapter! A poor diet can bring greater reactivity toward stress. Reaching for high-fat, high-sugar foods can provide a temporary sense of relief that adds to your long-term stress. Refined carbs, such as cookies and potato chips, can cause a spike in blood sugar. When your blood sugar crashes, you might experience more stress and anxiety. I, like most, enjoy a treat from time to time. And there's nothing wrong with that, within reason. If you make too many foods off-limits you will find it difficult to maintain those limitations in the long run. Try to enjoy those treats in moderation and in conjunction with a healthy diet, remembering that a healthy diet helps you combat stress over the long haul.

Seek out social support. Having supportive people in your life is the key to stress management. If you lack emotional support and friendship, it's important to get it. That may mean reaching out to your existing network, or confiding in a family member or distant friend who can help you. That may be awkward or difficult, but necessary. Be honest about how you are feeling; no one benefits from covering up their feelings. You may also need to expand your network. Join a law-school organization (it is easier than you think), attend a support group, or get professional help if you lack supportive people in your life. We will discuss this further in the next section on resilience as well.

Conquer imposter syndrome. If you, like many, are struggling under the weight of imposter syndrome, consider these strategies to try to keep it in check — keep going, you're not alone! Remember, "you [and your classmates] may both be putting on a front, since law school is also typically not an environment that smiles upon open expressions of vulnerability."[38]

- Remind yourself, you must have done something right to be here, and you have conquered challenges before. Reflect on those achievements.

- Understand that you are learning a completely new skill set and it may take some time for it to gel. I tell my students that regardless of their past success in writing, legal writing is like learning a new language. You would never expect to speak a new language fluently in the first few months you are learning it, would you? Cut yourself some slack, then, if Torts or any other subject does not immediately click for you.

- Internalize the idea that mistakes are a part of anything worth doing, and learn from them.

- Find a mentor. Use your career services office or rely on professors to help you find someone you may have something in common with. That mentor you look up to may have also suffered from imposter syndrome — or, if they haven't, they may be able to help you find perspective on your own feelings.

Make relaxation techniques part of your daily schedule. There are a number of relaxation techniques you can try. Not every technique is for everyone. But relaxation should be! Here are some suggestions:

- **Mindfulness.** We talked about mindfulness in the last chapter. Mindfulness techniques like breathing exercises or mindful walking or running are not only good for developing the focus for studying, they also help manage stress and therefore allow for better quality of life in general. One breathing technique, called 4-7-8 breathing, is particularly good for lessening anxiety. In moments of panic or shock, your breathing can become shallow, which results in a build-up of carbon dioxide, producing inflammation and acidification in the body. By slowing down your breath, holding it in, and then exhaling for a longer time, you can get rid of as much carbon dioxide as possible, and return your body to its equilibrium. Here is how you do it:

  - Place the tip of the tongue on the roof of the mouth (behind the front teeth).
  - Breathe in through the nose for a count of four.
  - Hold your breath for a count of seven.
  - Release the breath through your mouth with a whooshing sound for a count of eight.
  - Without a pause, repeat these steps another three or four times.
  - Then resume normal breathing.

- **Yoga.** Yoga combines physical movement, meditation, light exercise, and controlled breathing — all of which provide excellent stress relief. And while you're likely to reap immediate benefits from a single yoga session, you'll get long-term benefits if you incorporate it into your life in a consistent way. Yoga offers a variety of physical, psychological, and spiritual benefits. I found yoga intimidating when I first started. It helped me to stand in the back of the class until I felt more comfortable, but I also had to remind myself that it is okay to be vulnerable, or not know exactly what I am doing all the time. Online classes can also help you become confident enough to join a class. Yoga has been around for at least about 5,000 years, so it's a safe bet that it must be worthwhile.

- **Guided imagery.** This is like taking a short vacation in your mind. Imagine yourself in your "happy place" — maybe sitting on a beach, listening to the waves, smelling the ocean, and feeling the warm sand underneath you. Or, you can listen to someone walk you through a peaceful scene. Once you know how to do it yourself, you can practice guided imagery on your own. Simply close your eyes for a few moments and go to that happy place. Think about all the sensory experiences you'd engage in and allow yourself to feel as though you're really there. After a few minutes, open your eyes and return to the present moment.

- **Aromatherapy.** Aromatherapy has real benefits for stress relief — it can help you to feel energized, more relaxed, or more present in the moment. Emerging research suggests certain scents can alter brain wave activity and decrease stress hormones in the body. One reason aromatherapy can be so effective: it smells so nice that it makes you want to take a deeper breath, and that deeper breathing slows the nervous system and calms you. My personal favorite scent is lavender, which immediately takes me in my mind to the end of my yoga class where the teacher would use the scent to create a mood of relaxation. So, for me, lavender is particularly helpful because it combines guided imagery (my yoga class) and aromatherapy.

- **Laughter.** A good sense of humor can't cure all ailments, but data is mounting about the positive things laughter can do. A good laugh fires up and then cools down your stress response, and it can increase and then decrease your heart rate and blood pressure. The result? A good, relaxed feeling. In fact, a 2012 study found that smilers enjoyed lower heart rates during stress recovery and a smaller drop in positive emotions during stressful tasks.[39] Which reminds me: have you heard the one about the perfectionist who walked into a bar? Apparently, the bar wasn't set high enough. (I hope you are laughing, and I will also take this opportunity to remind you that perfectionism is unnecessarily stressful and counterproductive.)

- **Music.** Several studies have demonstrated the benefits of music on the body. Research has shown that listening to and playing music increases the body's production of the antibody immunoglobulin A and natural killer cells — the cells that attack invading viruses and boost the immune system's effectiveness. Music also reduces levels of the stress hormone cortisol. While the idea of music is similar to that of mantras, in that it produces an energy or a vibration that one becomes consumed in, the truth is not all music will elicit a calming effect. Listening to calming music you particularly like, or classical music, when stressed, can significantly reduce negative emotional states and physiological arousal compared to listening to heavy metal music or sitting in silence. As the music enters our ears and activates our brain, it helps stimulate reward pathways that are linked to positive emotions.

- **Positive affirmation.** The way you talk to yourself matters. Harsh self-criticism, self-doubt, and catastrophic predictions aren't helpful. If you're constantly thinking things like "I don't have time for this," and "I can't stand this," or "I'll never get an A," you'll stress yourself out. Try to talk to yourself in a more realistic, compassionate manner. When you doubt your ability to succeed, reply with a kinder inner dialogue. Positive self-talk can help you develop a healthier outlook. And an optimistic and compassionate conversation can help you manage your emotions and take positive action.

- **Gratitude.** Gratitude helps you recognize all the things you have to be thankful for. Whether you're grateful for a sunny day or thankful you arrived at school safely, think about all the good things you have in life. Gratitude also reminds you of all of the resources you have to cope with stress, which can be quite empowering. Studies show grateful people enjoy better mental health, lower stress, and a better quality of life. So, whether you decide to make it a habit to identify what you're grateful for as you sit around the dinner table or to write down three things you're grateful for in a gratitude journal every day, make gratitude a regular habit. But remember that all gratitude doesn't need to be saved for the journal. Tell the people in your life how much you appreciate them. From people in your family to sales clerks and postal employees you encounter in your day, everyone likes to know that they're appreciated. Their positive reactions can help put you in positive mood, too! Here are some simple suggestions for starting a journal.

  ○ **Decide on a type of journal that appeals to you.** You can write long, descriptive paragraphs about what you appreciate in your daily life, or, your journal can consist entirely of lists. You could set a preset number of items per entry per day (10 per day, for example). Or, you could decide on an amount of time to write every day and then just write whatever seems right for a particular day. You may want to maintain your journal online or in paper form. Do you want to type or print? If you spend all day on the computer, writing on paper may be a good change. Where will you write? In bed at night? Or is there another time of day or place that is better? Is privacy an issue? Your personal laptop may be best if you'd like to keep your thoughts private in your home.

  ○ **Commit to a schedule.** An important aspect of the long-term success of your gratitude journal is the frequency with which you use it. It's usually best to aim for once a day or several times per week in the beginning, but allow yourself some wiggle room if things get busy. You want to make a commitment that will keep you inspired to write, even if you aren't always in the mood, because this exercise can help *change* your mood. Don't make your schedule so rigid that you'll be tempted to give up the whole plan if you slip up once or twice. Even if you don't feel the rewards for some time, keep writing. Gratitude journals tend to be most effective when you write about three items at the end of each day. This is regular enough and simple enough to be doable and writing at the end of the day tends to bring the best benefits.

○ **Reflect on your journal.** Many people find that their whole attitude changes once they've been keeping a gratitude journal for a while. They tend to notice things throughout the day that they may want to include in the journal, things they wouldn't have otherwise noticed. Remember that you may want to read over your journal entries in the future. This can be a great pick-me-up when you're feeling stressed or depressed. Experiment with the types of things you write about. If you find yourself always mentioning the obvious things ("I'm grateful for my family") every day, challenge yourself to notice the subtle things ("Today I volunteered in Contracts!").

To sum it up, stress happens, especially in law school. You have chosen an educational path and a career that will cause it. Building healthy habits now will help you perform better in school, and help you develop coping mechanisms which will benefit you as you enter the legal profession. Commit to practicing healthy coping mechanisms now. Even if you are aware of stress and try to handle it, there may come a time that you suffer drawbacks or obstacles. Dealing with those situations requires resilience, which we will discuss in the next section.

Stop and Reflect:
Tackle Your Stress

1. Consider the three things you identified in the last in section that are causing you stress and list three tips offered in this chapter you can try.

Guided Imagery
listen to music
Laughter

2. How will you implement the three tips you plan to try? Be specific. Remember, planning and scheduling are two key ways to reduce stress.

when ever I feel stressed I'll
try doing one of the things listed

CHAPTER FOUR

Resilience

*In any case you mustn't confuse a single failure
with a final defeat.*

F. SCOTT FITZGERALD

esilience is a bit of a buzzword right now, isn't it? But the concept of resilience has been around a long time. It's hard to read anything about learning, or stress, without also reading about resilience. But what is resilience? It is essentially a set of skills — as opposed to a disposition or personality type — that make it possible for people not only to get through hard times but to thrive during and after them.[40]

Neuroscientists are actively studying resilience to better understand why some people bounce back from difficult experiences while others do not. Thanks to modern imaging, scientists can actually see inside the brain to the parts that govern emotion and understand how stress changes the structure and functioning of the brain. By observing blood flow patterns, they can see how different people react to stress. Like animals whose pulse quickly returns to normal after escaping a predator, resilient brains can more quickly shut down the stress responses, such as the pumping of cortisol, our bodies engage in and return to normal more quickly.

Now you know that in today's world, it doesn't take a predator to trigger this kind of stress response: we can be triggered by exams, grades, family situations, and even feelings of social pain like rejection and loneliness. Basically, a host of reasons can trigger the physiological responses of our evolutionary ancestors. And the more we worry, the more we activate the worry neurons in our brains and the more it can become a cycle. Remember the connection between the prefrontal cortex, where executive functioning happens, and the amygdala, the emotional part of the brain that responds to threats? The stronger the connection between them, the better the prefrontal cortex is at shutting the amygdala down.

Scientists proved this theory with experiments on a group of Navy SEALs, who were able to calm their emotional responses quickly. Brain imaging showed that the SEALs could more easily jump between different emotions, indicating that their prefrontal cortex could control the amygdala better than the average person, proving their resilience.[41] Of course, Navy SEALs undergo vigorous training to work on this trait. In fact, their published Ethos states:

> I will never quit. I persevere and thrive on adversity. My Nation expects me to be physically harder and mentally stronger than my enemies. If knocked down, I will get back up, every time. I will draw on every remaining ounce of strength to protect my teammates and to accomplish our mission. I am never out of the fight.[42]

The good news is that you don't have to be a Navy SEAL to learn to tamp down your emotional responses. Just like working your biceps or abs, training your brain can build up strength in the right places at the right times too. Resilience is not a fixed state. You may be more resilient at different times in your life than others. Most importantly, resilience can be learned, practiced, developed, and strengthened.

Tips for Building Resilience
(or, grow through what you go through)

You will notice that many of the suggestions for building your resilience are also covered in other chapters. Here, more than ever, it becomes apparent just how much all of the core elements of brain health and wellness depend upon and reinforce one another.

Build and cultivate your social connections. Social connection improves physical health and psychological wellbeing. A lack of social connection is worse for your physical health than obesity, smoking, and high blood pressure.[43] What's more, loneliness is an emotional stressor, and it takes a toll on the endocrine, cardiovascular, and immune systems. That damage is even greater when you are going through a particularly tough time. Our brains are wired such that when we face difficult circumstances, we use more metabolic resources if we are alone. On the flip side, strong social connection leads to increased chances of longevity.[44] Social connection strengthens the immune system, helps us recover from disease faster, and may even lead to longer lives. People who feel more connected to others have lower rates of anxiety and depression, and also have higher self-esteem and are more empathic to others, more trusting, and more cooperative; as a consequence, others are more open to trusting and cooperating with them. Social connectedness therefore generates a positive feedback loop of social, emotional, and physical wellbeing. Unfortunately, a lack of social connections has generally been associated with declines in physical and psychological health as well as a higher propensity to antisocial behavior, which leads to further isolation. So clearly, social connection has great physical and mental benefits.

How can you build your social connections? This can be challenging if you find yourself in a new environment, away from your home or your college friends. Here are some suggestions:

Be engaged in the law school community; don't just be a spectator. Most people feel lonely or isolated at times during law school, even if they don't show it. Remember that many students may feel like imposters, and that you are not alone.

- Find ways to connect with other students in meaningful ways, perhaps through a study group or review session. If you are studying online, set up a Zoom social hour with classmates. (Just remember all the Zoom fatigue tips, please.)

- What areas of law interest you? Join student organizations involving those topics. Attend functions or listen to speakers your school sponsors on those topics. You'll not only meet others with common interests but you'll also learn more about your interests.

- What classes, clinics, or other law school experiences have you particularly enjoyed?

  o What about those experiences appealed to you? The subject matter? Professor? Colleagues?

  o Try to connect with the professors of those classes about your interest in the area, and to identify other course offerings or activities that may help you further that interest.

  o What does your interest in this area mean for your career path? Consult your academic advisor or career services office for advice on networking in this area.

- Volunteer. Many local bar associations or public interest groups welcome volunteers.

- Start conversations, ask questions, and be an active listener. Don't just bury your head in your books.

- Get to know your professors or TA's. They are there to help and genuinely enjoy talking with students outside of class. Go to office hours or extra review sessions; you'll get to meet more people and you will advance your learning. I know that

I enjoy getting to know my students outside of the class-room, and welcome that opportunity to learn more about their interests.

Try to build connections outside of law school as well. Try not to limit your universe to your law school contacts. Realize that others also feel lonely or isolated, and even casual contacts with others are energizing and uplifting.

- Even fleeting moments of connection can have an impact. Take a moment to say hello to people as you go through your day — the woman who serves you coffee, the cashier at the grocery store, your neighbor or classmate. Ask how that person is and really listen to the response.

- Increase your opportunities to interact with others. Try an activity at the community center, take an exercise class, join a spiritual group, or go for a walk in the mall, your neighborhood, or around school. I find I meet and connect with countless people when I walk my dog. Just being out in my neighborhood means I increase the chances of interacting with others, and these small and brief connections are surprisingly enjoyable. If you don't have a dog, offer to walk someone else's! We dog owners are always looking for help.

- Become involved in something larger than yourself. Work at the food pantry, visit a friend or acquaintance who's lonely or ill, offer to help someone carry their groceries to the car, give up your seat on the bus or in a waiting area, let someone in front of you in line.

- Share from your own experiences. Consider what you might like from others to help you feel more connected, and offer this to someone else — a friend, family member, classmate, or neighbor. Perhaps you can invite someone to lunch or make an impromptu phone call. Reaching out like this is particularly gratifying as you can appreciate that you have something to offer while also making social connections.

Practice self-awareness and self-care. Self-awareness is your capacity to clearly understand your own strengths, weaknesses, emotions, values, natural inclinations, tendencies, and motivation. Self-care refers to behaviors, thoughts, and attitudes that support your emotional wellbeing and physical health. It is difficult to bounce back from setbacks if you are not taking proper care of your mental and physical needs. We are all very good at finding and dwelling on our perceived faults and weaknesses. Consider how you probably give others the benefit of the doubt, or see them more positively then they may see themselves. One of my children is particularly hard on himself, but very kind and accepting of others. I always encourage him to try to view himself as he is willing to view others. Where he will easily identify and appreciate others' strengths while easily accepting their weakness, he downplays his own strengths and focuses only on his weaknesses. Why should we be less kind or understanding of ourselves than we are to others?

Here are some other suggestions for practicing self-awareness and self-care, most of which are also covered in depth in other chapters as well:

- Identify what makes you special. We all have strengths and weaknesses. Try not to focus only on the weaknesses, but rather embrace your strengths as well.

- Practice self-compassion. Having compassion for yourself is really no different from having compassion for others. Self-compassion involves acting the same way towards yourself when you are having a difficult time, fail, or notice something you don't like about yourself. Instead of just ignoring your pain with a "stiff upper lip" mentality, stop to tell yourself "this is really difficult right now," and ask, "how can I comfort and care for myself in this moment?"

- Make time for quiet reflection through meditation, prayer, journaling, yoga, spending time in nature, or practicing gratitude.

- Don't forget to have fun! You cannot be one-dimensional, only focusing on school, and expect to be healthy.

Think bigger than yourself to find meaning. Finding meaning is the act of making sense of—and exploring the significance of—an experience or situation. Research shows that cultivating a sense of meaning in your life can contribute more to positive mental health than pursuing happiness. Researchers have found that developing an ethical code to guide daily decisions can help build resiliency.

- Examine your strengths and talents, develop skills you want, recognize your values, pursue interests and passions, and live your own unique combination of these.

- Find ways to help others. Maybe you can combine your legal interests and talents to volunteer for an organization that helps others.

- Keep a long-term perspective and consider stressors in a broader context. Try not to get stuck on a particular grade, professor, course, or experience.

- Reflect on what's going well and what's not. Albert Einstein is widely credited with saying, "[t]he definition of insanity is doing the same thing over and over again, but expecting different results." Stop and assess what is working for you academically and socially and what isn't. If something isn't going well, make changes.

- Explore spiritual or religious practices that fit your world view and values. Some suggestions include:

  o Find a local church you can attend which matches your interests.

  o Read books and engage in conversations about the meaning of life.

- ○ Enjoy the natural world, for example, gardening or hiking, watching sunsets, travelling to scenic places, spending time at a cottage, savoring the first snowfall or spring buds.

- ○ Try to live ethically, by integrating justice and fairness, peace-making, or green practices into your life.

- Strive to accept what you cannot change; make conscious choices to act where you can influence a process, outcome, or relationship.

Adopt a "growth mindset." Cultivating a "growth mindset" is a very important part of building resilience. It is the opposite of a "fixed mindset," when you believe that your intelligence and abilities are fixed, innate traits that you can't change. Instead, a "growth mindset" acknowledges that you can learn from challenges, and through these experiences can increase your intellect and abilities. Understand that the study and practice of law will inevitably mean that you will face setbacks and challenges and that you cannot let those setbacks negatively impact your view of yourself. I know that this is challenging in law school, when competition and the grading curve can make it very difficult to focus on learning rather than the grade. Try to remind yourself this is a temporary condition, but that the knowledge and skills gained in law school will stay with you throughout your career.

On a personal note, I always share with my students that I got a C in Torts my first year of law school. I tell them that I know how it feels to doubt yourself, wonder if you are good enough, feel the pressure of the 1L year, and even to question your decision to go to law school or be a lawyer. I also share that it took well into my 2L year before I felt things turn around, and I don't believe that to be unusual. It can be hard to have that perspective when you are in the midst of mid-terms or finals or memo deadlines, but try. You will be building resiliency for your future practice of law, where you will inevitably face cases you lose, clients who are left unhappy, supervisors who expect too much, judges who are always difficult, and other challenges and circumstances beyond your control. Here are a few more specific tips to build your growth mindset:

- Leave the "genius" myth behind — achievement requires hard work, not just natural talent.

- Focus on "brain training" — your brain is like a muscle that needs to work to get stronger. Good for you for reading this book!

- Prioritize learning over memorizing, and the process over the end result. I know this is easier said than done, but it's important and you should try.

- View challenges and setbacks as opportunities to grow, to learn something new.

- Avoid comparing yourself to others — we all have different strengths and learn differently. Grading curves and the competition inherent in law school and the practice of law make this difficult. But that is precisely why building resilience is so important: you need it.

- Don't dwell on the past or beat yourself up over things you wish you had done better. Learn from those experiences and move on. I had to get over my C, and you will get over your disappointments, too. I became keenly aware of my weakness in taking multiple choice exams. I knew that I needed to work on that to prepare for the bar exam, and I did. Maybe I wouldn't have studied as much or as well for the bar if I had not suffered that result in Torts. You, too, will certainly face disappointments in law school, so try to focus on what you learned by going through the process or event.

Get help. What if you are still struggling? It happens, and there are many resources law students and lawyers can turn to for help. You shouldn't hesitate to seek them out; in fact, you should take advantage of the free resources available to you. You are training to be an advocate for your clients, so first, practice advocating for yourself by seeking help if you need it. No one gains from your keeping your stress or anxiety to yourself, especially you. You don't need to go it alone, you don't need to pretend like everything is fine if it's not, and you shouldn't feel ashamed asking for help when you need it. It's also important to remember that getting professional treatment for mental health and even substance abuse does not appear on bar fitness results. So, if you're struggling, please do not wait to get help.

Use your law school resources. Most if not all law schools have at least two primary places you can turn to for help: the dean of students and the office of student services. Most dean of students' offices help with personal and academic matters. The office of student services typically offers counseling, including mental health, substance abuse, and wellness. These offices are a safe, confidential space with an open-door policy, available to all students from the day you begin. They understand law school can be stressful and therefore provide a myriad of resources and helpful programming, including things like:

- Peer health education programs.
- Free and confidential counseling for alcohol and drugs.
- Resources on topics like stress, sleep, sexual health, alcohol, and other drugs, both legal and illegal.

Familiarize yourself with these resources so that you know where to turn if needed before it is an emergency. And remember, don't be afraid to reach out.

Connect with the Lawyer Assistance Program of your state bar. The Lawyer Assistance Programs ("LAP") of each state bar offer a wide variety of programs, including programs and services that are offered virtually or by telephone. The American Bar Association maintains a comprehensive list of LAP websites and contact information.[45] LAPs offer programs that cover many wellbeing angles, including substance abuse, mental health, time management, and loneliness in the profession. Services include: confidential telephone calls with licensed counselors; assessment and referral services to treatment programs; ongoing counseling; and virtual events.

The ABA has compiled helpful resources which are easily accessible in a publication titled *Substance Use and Mental Health Toolkit for Law School Students and Those Who Care About Them: A Collaborative Effort of the ABA Law Student Division and the ABA Commission on Lawyer Assistance Programs (CoLAP).*[46]

Talk to someone now

- National Suicide Prevention Hotline: 1-800-273-8255
- Crisis Text Line: Text "Home" to 741741 for immediate help
- Lawlifeline.org
- Veteran's Crisis Line: Call 1-800-273-8255 and Press 1, or text 838255

STOP

Stop and Reflect:
If at First You Don't Succeed, Then What?

Think of a time you suffered a setback, whether it was academic or personal.

1. How did you handle it and how did it affect you moving forward?

   I was disappointed but
   rebounded quickly to try again
   2nd attempt wasnt perfect
   but was better

2. What would you tell yourself if you could go back to that time?

   I know this sucks right
   now but you'll get through it
   and ya'll be better for it

3. What can you learn from looking back at that experience to apply to challenges you face now?

   That not letting yourself
   feel defeated and useless
   is important

CHAPTER FIVE

Exercise

When it comes to health and wellbeing, regular exercise
is about as close to a magic potion as you can get.

THICH NHAT HANH

Perhaps you are surprised to find that a law school textbook has a chapter on exercise. You already know my personal view of it. And you likely know that exercise is good for your body, but did you also know how good it is for your brain? By now, you know from earlier chapters that exercise helps improve cognitive function, enhance alertness, and reduce levels of stress. People tend to exercise to stay fit and ward off physical conditions like heart disease, diabetes, and high blood pressure. Some people exercise to lose or maintain their weight. Most people don't work out specifically to improve their cognitive functioning, but perhaps they should. Exercise improves cognitive functioning, mental health, and memory; it also hinders the development of certain neurological conditions. We can probably agree that as a law student, anything that improves cognitive functioning, mental health, and memory is something you should probably be doing, right? Moreover, a growing number of studies support the idea that physical exercise is a lifestyle factor that might lead to increased physical and mental health throughout life. Now you can see why we need a whole chapter on exercise.

Your Brain Loves the Gym

Exercise is so good for you in so many ways that I could write a whole book on it. Not only does it improve your physical and mental abilities, but being active also gives you more energy during the day and helps you sleep better at night. In turn, and as we learned in the section on focus, better sleep improves creativity and overall brain function. Exercise also boosts mood and reduces stress. When you exercise, your body releases chemicals known as dopamine and endorphins that make you feel happy (runner's high, anyone?). Not only is your brain pumping out these feel-good chemicals, but exercise also helps your brain get rid of chemicals which make you feel stressed or anxious. People who exercise tend

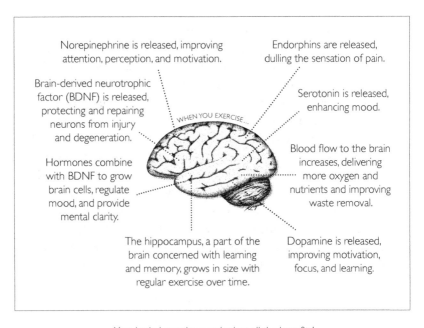

Norepinephrine is released, improving attention, perception, and motivation.

Endorphins are released, dulling the sensation of pain.

Brain-derived neurotrophic factor (BDNF) is released, protecting and repairing neurons from injury and degeneration.

WHEN YOU EXERCISE...

Serotonin is released, enhancing mood.

Hormones combine with BDNF to grow brain cells, regulate mood, and provide mental clarity.

Blood flow to the brain increases, delivering more oxygen and nutrients and improving waste removal.

The hippocampus, a part of the brain concerned with learning and memory, grows in size with regular exercise over time.

Dopamine is released, improving motivation, focus, and learning.

Your brain loves the gym: look at all the benefits!

to be happier and less stressed than those who don't exercise. Regular exercise can help you control your emotions when you do feel angry or upset. I could go on, but I'm sure you get my point.

To better understand how exercise helps the brain, it's helpful to understand what is happening in the body and brain during exercise. As you exercise and your heart rate increases, blood flow to the brain increases and more oxygen and nutrients go there. Exercise also induces the release of beneficial proteins in the brain. These nourishing proteins keep brain cells, called neurons, healthy, and promote the growth of new neurons. Neurons are the building blocks of the brain, and every single one is important to overall brain health.

There are three main neuroscientific theories that explain how physical activity positively impacts cognition:

1. While exercising, oxygen saturation and angiogenesis (blood vessel growth) occur in areas of the brain associated with rational thinking as well as social, physical, and intellectual performance.

2. Exercise causes stress hormones to drop and increases the number of neurotransmitters like serotonin and norepinephrine, which are known to accelerate information processing.

3. Exercise upregulates neurotrophins (brain-derived neurotrophic factor, insulin-like growth factor, and basic fibroblast growth factor). These support the survival and differentiation of neurons in the developing brain, dendritic branching, and synaptic machinery in the adult brain.[47]

That's all a bit technical, but suffice to say, scientific research shows various ways in which exercise impacts the brain in that it affects neurogenesis (creates new neurons), neuroplasticity (improves how existing neurons work), and neurochemistry (releases neurotransmitters that improve brain function).[48] While these theories differ slightly, the bottom line is that exercise directly improves brain functioning. And what law student would not want to improve that?

To understand the physiology of the brain and connection to exercise, let's think about how our brains developed. Before the industrial age, humans expended significant energy in their daily lives in farming and other labor-intensive work. The modern age resulted in a "leisure revolution," where technology quickened production lines and decreased the number of active jobs for the rising middle class. People became more sedentary, and pastimes like TV watching, and now, internet surfing, became the norm. Today, daily life revolves around multiple screens, large to small, and much of our lives is conducted online. Without any real physical effort, we can go about our daily lives: attending class, working, paying bills, and shopping online means we don't even walk around shopping aisles or commute anymore. Seventy-five percent of the United States population fails to meet even the minimum government recommendation for exercise, that is, 30 minutes walking every day. Compare that to the habits of our hunter-gatherer ancestors 10,000 years ago, who walked at least five to ten miles every day.[49] Now, I am not suggesting that we need to go to that extreme, but the bottom line is "we are not genetically programmed to live in this state of idleness and lethargy . . . and if we do, our brains pay a high price, both in the short term and the long term."[50]

Let's pause here to reflect on the effect of a sedentary state coupled with constant distraction. Remember that when distraction interrupts focus, the part of the brain our ancestors relied on to deal with immediate dangers, the "fight or flight" response, is activated. And that part of the brain detracts from the work of the prefrontal cortex used in deep focus. Now think about how the lack of exercise also relates to our ancestral tendencies. We activate the "fight or flight" response with 24/7 access to technology but we don't actually "fly," that is, we don't generate the increased blood flow that would be beneficial to the brain. That's a lose-lose, isn't it? Bottom line: the worst thing you can do for your brain is to not exercise but remain distracted.

How much and what kind of exercise is best? I have always taken the position that any exercise is better than no exercise. And especially after researching for this book, I stand by that. I told you in the preface that I faced major setbacks in the years leading up to writing this book. Despite those challenges, the one thing I clung to every day was my workout schedule. Typically, I walk my dog twice a day, go to classes at the gym that include high-intensity interval training and strength training, and run on days I do not go to the gym. The pandemic forced me to change that schedule, but I kept up the exercise. People have asked me how I handled all of the challenges I faced, and my most honest answer is exercise. It gave me purpose every morning, it kept my blood going, and my endorphins flowing. It helped me keep and build social connections, and, most probably, staved off depression. While this schedule works for me, I am not suggesting that everyone needs to commit to it, or to the types of exercise I enjoy. I am suggesting that you need some type of regular exercise in your life. If you do not regularly exercise, it may seem daunting to start. And exercise could start off feeling a little like a chore, something that you have to do. But unlike actual chores, it is something that will become fun and possibly even irresistible if you keep it up.

- **Aerobic exercise.** A wealth of studies both in humans and animals have linked the cognitive improvements following aerobic exercise, such as running and cycling, to the increased capacity of the heart, lungs, and blood to transport oxygen. This results in generalized brain effects, like a boost in the number of blood vessels and synapses, increasing brain volume, and decreasing age-related brain atrophy. Aside from this, more localized effects in brain areas related to thinking and problem-solving have also been reported, such as a boost in the number of new nerve cells and increases in proteins that help these neurons survive and thrive.

- **Resistance and weight training.** Cognitive improvements have also been demonstrated with other forms of exercise, such as low-intensity mind-body exercises like yoga and tai chi and resistance or weight training. Because these exercises either do not work the heart as hard, or do so in a different way, less is known about how they promote cognitive changes. Most experts recommend a combination of cardiovascular and strength training, for all of the other benefits exercise bestows on both mind and body. In addition to improving your brain function, you should expect to see improvements in cardiorespiratory fitness and muscle strength, as well as reducing the risk of obesity, diabetes, and hypertension, among other diseases. These types of exercise are also important to our overall health. If you are not used to exercising, you may need to start with a gentler routine, eventually building up to more vigorous exercise practices.

You don't have to be a fitness fanatic to reap all of the benefits of exercise. Research indicates that modest amounts of exercise can make a difference. The American Heart Association recommends, at a minimum, 150 minutes of moderate exercise or 75 minutes of vigorous exercise a week. Brain researchers suggest 45 minutes to an hour of moderate-to-vigorous exercise as good for the brain. If you don't already exercise, then start by adding a little exercise to your routine, in small intervals at first. The secret is not the quantity, but rather the consistency and frequency of the movement.

If you are looking to target and enhance a specific element of brain health through exercise, the following list may come in handy:

- For brain fog and concentration: yoga, tai chi, and aerobic classes

- For memory: aerobics, walking, and cycling

- To improve blood circulation: cardio activities (walking, riding a bicycle, running swimming, kickboxing, skipping rope, and skiing)

- For stress and anxiety: yoga and weight training
- And for depression: aerobic and resistance training[51]

Remember, think of your brain as a muscle. If you don't care for it, some of its parts will shrink and their function will deteriorate. To optimize their capacity, you have to continuously train them and push them further each time. Commit to exercise as a habit, like attending a review session or taking a prescription medication, and both your brain and body will benefit.

Tips to Start or Maintain an Exercise Routine
(or, good things come to those who sweat)

If you are not already committed to an exercise routine, or even if you are, law school and its many deadlines and stresses can make it easy to talk yourself out of exercising. You have to think about exercising as being good for your brain, good for studying, and therefore a worthy use of your time, even during exams or other deadlines. Schedule it like you would a study session so you don't skip it.

Here are some tips to get you started or keep you going:

Find your own internal motivation. Studies show that people who work out because they recognize the internal benefits and love it, rather than to look good for a class reunion or other special event, are the ones who tend to stick with it in the long run. It's easy to see why. Like going on a diet to drop pounds for a special event (and then the bingeing that may come after), exercise geared to the event and not the overall benefit to you is not likely to last.

Take small steps. You can't go from never running to suddenly running five miles, or not being a biker to biking 20 miles. If you do too much, too soon, you'll end up sore, injured, or very discouraged. Try a little at a time, working up to your goal. Research shows this is the best way to build a heathy habit.

Keep at it. Even if your form isn't perfect, you feel self-conscious, or you wish you were better, don't give up. No one is perfect to start. In fact, this is probably a good time to remind you that no one is ever perfect, in anything! (Not even the perfectionist...hahaha.)

Mix up your workouts. Doing different kinds of workouts will keep you interested. We all know someone who picked up a new interest: say they joined a boxing gym, and then boxed every day, raving about how much they love it. (You might sense that this is a real person in my life. Thankfully, it's someone unlikely to read this book.) You know when you listen to them talk that it's only a matter of time before they stop because it will become too much, or they will get injured, or bored. And yes, my boxing friend is no longer boxing. Overdoing one form of exercise is counterproductive to your overall health. Instead, mix things up. If running is usually your thing, try some biking or swimming. Or switch between types of strength training so that you're not working the same muscles again and again. Both your brain and body will stay more engaged, and you will be much more likely to stick to it.

Try having a workout partner (or don't). Maybe you're the kind of person who works out better if you have a partner to hold you accountable. Or maybe, like me, you enjoy solo running because it allows you to meditate or think through problems. Or maybe you like a little of both. Studies generally show that you work out longer if you have a pal or you join a class. But a combination of both may be best.

Don't let the clock intimidate you. Remember that the American Heart Association recommends 150 minutes of moderate exercise or 75 minutes of vigorous exercise a week. Health experts also recommend two to three days of weight training for all the benefits beyond heart health. If you find this difficult to fit into your schedule, remember that you can break up your exercise into 10- or 15-minute sessions. Go for a power walk to take a break from your studying, walk to get a cup of coffee, do jumping jacks and jog in place...you get the idea. Remember we learned in an earlier chapter that breaking up your intense focus with an exercise break is good for your focus, too.

Be consistent. Working out should become part of your routine and you should schedule it into your days. When it is part of your routine, you won't even have to think about it. And once it is routine, your mind and body will crave the release it offers and the productivity it unleashes!

Use a fitness journal. Or an app. It is rewarding to be able to reflect on your progress. You'll feel more accountable to yourself, too. You will see that the sample daily and weekly schedules, as well as the wellness tracker in the Appendix, all contain a place to plan and record your exercise.

Reward yourself! Exercise can have benefits like medication, but the results do not occur overnight. It can take weeks to feel real change, so reward yourself by going out with friends, etc., to keep yourself motivated in the meantime.

Stop and Reflect:
Fit Happens

Try using a fitness journal to monitor and track your exercise. You can make your own, download free examples from the internet, or buy a commercial journal. There are many options. Regardless of which you try, look at a week at time and plan a variety of cardio and strength-training workouts. Remember, though, that choosing to take the stairs instead of the elevator, or walking with a friend to get coffee instead of sitting on the sofa, also counts towards your overall fitness!

_____

_____

_____

_____

_____

_____

_____

_____

_____

_____

_____

_____

_____

_____

CHAPTER SIX

Sleep

*It is a common experience that a problem difficult at night
is resolved in the morning after the committee of sleep
has worked on it.*

JOHN STEINBECK

Sleep. It sounds simple, yet sleep is an incredibly complex physiological process that involves virtually all of the body's systems. Sleep is as essential to your survival as food and water. You probably recall blissful sleep in your not-so-distant past, sleep that came easily, lasted long, and left you feeling refreshed. Maybe you've never given sleep much thought or maybe you are currently sleep deprived as you navigate the stresses of law school. Considering its vital importance to both your physical and mental wellbeing, and therefore your ability to be most effective in studying and later for your clients — and the fact that we spend about half of our lives sleeping or trying to — it merits our attention.

While there are no official national guidelines for sleep, many organizations suggest adults get seven to nine hours a night. Sleep consists of four stages,[52] each essential to the regenerative process:

- **Stage one** occurs at the onset of sleep when you are transitioning from wakefulness to sleep. This stage lasts minutes and you are easily awoken. Brain waves are still quite active during this stage.

- **Stage two** lasts about 20 minutes. During this phase, brain waves become slower, respiratory and heart rates slow, and your body temperature declines. This is still considered a "light sleep" phase, though you may spend 40 to 50% of your time in this stage of sleep.

- **Stage three** is known as "slow wave" sleep, and it is the beginning of the deeper sleep phase. Blood pressure falls, breathing slows further, and body temperature continues to decline. People are harder to awaken from this phase.

- **Stage four** is REM sleep. It takes about 90 minutes to enter this phase, and you may enter it repeatedly throughout the night, totaling about one and a half to two hours. Your brain becomes more active during this phase, and eyes tend to move rapidly as you dream. Heart rate and blood pressure increase and breathing becomes irregular, faster, and shallower. In this stage, the brain consolidates and processes what it learned the day before, preparing the brain to store information in its long-term memory.

In the past, scientists were not clear what our brains do during sleep. Now researchers have evidence that a good night's sleep may literally clear the mind. Researchers found that the space surrounding brain cells — called the interstitial space — may increase during sleep, allowing the brain to flush out toxins that build up during waking hours.[53] Previous research shows that proteins linked to neurodegenerative diseases build up in that space. Now it is believed that the restorative function of sleep may be due to the switching of the brain into a state that facilitates the clearance of waste products that accumulate during wakefulness. Brain cells are highly sensitive to their environment. Toxins can interfere with nerve function and damage cells, so it's essential to quickly and efficiently remove waste products from the interstitial space. Sleep is key to this process.

Sleep is essential to other processes as well. Sleep plays a role in the consolidation of memory, which is essential for learning new information. Without sufficient sleep, as we have already discussed, you may find it difficult to concentrate or learn new things. You may be impatient, have mood swings, find it challenging to remember new information, and your creativity will likely be compromised. "The bottom line is that sleep deprivation has a major impact on basic function from reaction time to memory to mood...In addition, chronic sleep deprivation is strongly correlated with behavioral health issues, such as depression, anxiety, substance abuse, and attempted suicide."[54] Not a good setup for a law student or lawyer working on behalf of a client, right? Law school and lawyering are stressful endeavors. Lack of sleep will only compound your stress.

Sleep also impacts the processes that help keep the heart and blood vessels healthy, including regulating your blood sugar, blood pressure, and inflammation levels. As we will discuss later, high blood sugar dampens your ability to concentrate, so sleep is good for your brain, your heart, and your overall health.

Moreover, sleep deprivation is a risk factor for becoming overweight or obese because of sleep's impact on two key hormones, leptin and ghrelin, which affect feelings of hunger and fullness.[55] (Poor diet choices and lack of exercise also play a role.) Lack of sleep can trigger a vicious cycle of overeating due to hormonal imbalances, or because of impaired decision making and impulse control. Lack of sleep can also lead to weight gain due to decreasing energy levels making it harder to be motivated and follow through on exercise. It can also prompt the body to release increased insulin, leading to higher blood sugar, which dampens your ability to concentrate.

A sleep diary can be a very helpful tool to track your sleep time and patterns. Used in sleep research and clinical settings, a sleep diary is a handy reference to help you become familiar with your own natural patterns of sleep and wakefulness. The information that you will record in the sleep diary is simple and straightforward. It includes the time you go to bed, the time you wake up, your total hours of sleep, and whether you had any nighttime awakenings (and if so, how long you were awake) and any daytime naps. In addition, note how you feel when you wake up — refreshed or tired — and how you feel at different times of the day. This will help you become more aware of your patterns and determine if you are getting adequate sleep. Just keeping track of your sleep in this way may help improve your situation. You can also use various apps to track your sleep. But, a word of caution here: when I tried using my watch to monitor my sleep, I found it stressed me out to wake up and have it tell me I had slept less than I thought I had. So, no more sleep apps for me. But I will share other tips which have worked for me, and more, in the next section.

Stop and Reflect:
Dear Diary, How's My Sleep?

Monitor your sleep for seven days. Record:

- The time you went to bed and woke up.
- How long and well you slept.
- When you were awake during the night.
- How much caffeine or alcohol you consumed and when.
- What and when you ate and drank.
- What emotion or stress you had.
- What drugs or medication you took.
- What exercise you had during the day and at what time.

What did you learn about your sleep habits?

_____

_____

_____

_____

_____

_____

_____

_____

_____

_____

_____

_____

Tips for Sleeping Better

(or, you snooze, you don't lose)

What gets in the way of good sleep? You may not have thought of this before, either because you have always had the good fortune of being a good sleeper, or because you didn't know what to do about it. Even if you have not suffered sleep issues before, you may find that the stresses of law school or practice will begin to affect you. Let's talk about how to improve sleep.

Paying attention to sleep is one of the most straightforward ways to set yourself up to sleep better. Give thought to having both a bedroom environment and daily routines that promote consistent, uninterrupted sleep. Keeping a stable sleep schedule, making your bedroom comfortable and free of disruptions, following a relaxing pre-bed routine, and building healthy habits during the day can all contribute to better sleep. Every sleeper can tailor their practices to suit their needs; certainly, one process does not fit all. Most important is that you harness positive habits to make it easier to sleep soundly throughout the night and wake up well-rested.

Here are some tips to help in each of these areas, but remember, they are not requirements. Adapt them to help you get the best sleep possible.

- **Set a sleep schedule.** Having a set schedule normalizes sleep as an essential part of your day and gets your brain and body accustomed to getting the amount of sleep you need. (You may be concluding that schedules, in general, are beneficial. You would be right.)

- **Have a fixed wake-up time.** Regardless of whether it's a weekday or weekend, try to wake up at the same time since a fluctuating schedule keeps you from getting into a rhythm of consistent sleep.

- **Prioritize sleep.** It might be tempting to skip sleep in order to work, study, socialize, or exercise, but it's vital to treat sleep as a priority. Remember that lack of sleep leads to an inability to focus and concentrate, so you're likely not achieving much academically by sacrificing sleep for study. Calculate a target bedtime based on your fixed wake-up time and do your best to be ready for bed around that time each night.

- **Make gradual adjustments.** If you want to shift your sleep times, don't try to do it all in one fell swoop because that can throw your schedule out of whack and confuse your body. Instead, make small, step-by-step adjustments, say a half hour or hour at a time, so that you can get adjusted and settle into a new schedule.

- **Don't overdo naps.** Naps can be a handy way to regain energy during the day, but they can throw off sleep at night. To avoid this, try to keep naps relatively short, half an hour or less, and limited to early afternoon.

- **Follow a nightly routine.** How you prepare for bed can determine how easily you'll be able to fall asleep. A pre-sleep playbook including some of these tips can put you at ease and make it easier to get to fall asleep when you want to.

- **Keep your routine consistent.** Following the same steps each night, including things like putting on your pajamas and brushing your teeth, can reinforce in your mind that it's bedtime.

- **Budget 30 minutes for winding down.** Take advantage of whatever puts you in a state of calm such as soft music, light stretching, reading, and relaxation exercises. Experiment with some of the relaxation techniques you read about in the chapter called Stress.

- **Dim your lights.** Avoid bright lights because they can hinder the production of the sleep hormone melatonin, which facilitates sleep.

- **Unplug.** Build in 30 to 60 device-free minutes before bed. Cell phones, tablets, and laptops stimulate you mentally and also generate blue light which may decrease melatonin production.

- **Try different ways to relax.** Instead of making falling asleep your goal, it's often easier to focus on relaxation. Meditation, mindfulness, paced breathing, and other relaxation techniques can put you in the right mindset for bed.

- **Don't toss and turn.** It helps to have a healthy mental connection between being in bed and actually being asleep. For that reason, if after 20 minutes you haven't gotten to sleep, get up and stretch, read, or do something else calming in low light before trying to fall asleep again.

There are other things you can do to promote sleep which you may not automatically think of as related to sleep. Incorporating healthy routines during the day can support your body's natural rhythms and limit sleep disruptions. These were touched on in other chapters as well, as each of these also promotes a healthy, agile brain.

- **Get daylight exposure.** Light, especially natural light, is one of the key drivers of circadian rhythms that can encourage quality sleep.

- **Be physically active.** Regular exercise can make for better sleep and also delivers a host of other health benefits you read about in the last chapter.

- **Don't smoke.** Nicotine stimulates the body in ways that disrupt sleep, which helps explain why smoking is correlated with many sleeping problems. Of course, there are any number of reasons why you shouldn't smoke, and absolutely zero reasons you should.

- **Don't overdrink.** You may feel that alcohol makes it easier to fall asleep, but the effect wears off, disrupting sleep later in the night. As a result, it's best to moderate alcohol consumption and avoid drinking alcohol later in the evening.

- **Cut down on caffeine late in the day:** Caffeine is a stimulant and can keep you wired even when you want to rest, so try to avoid it later in the day. Also avoid relying on caffeine to make up for a lack of sleep, lest you get caught in a vicious circle of caffeine overconsumption causing difficulty sleeping, leading to increased caffeine consumption, etc. Caffeine takes a certain amount of time — known as the "half-life" — to work through your system and be metabolized by your liver. One study showed that the half-life of caffeine in healthy adults is 5.7 hours.[56] This means if you consume 200 mg of caffeine (one to two cups of coffee) at mid-day, you would still have 100 mg in you at around 5:45 p.m. Pay attention to how caffeine affects you so that you don't sacrifice sleep by consuming too much.

- **Avoid eating late.** Eating dinner late, particularly a big, heavy, or spicy meal, can mean you're still digesting when it's time for bed. In general, any food or snacks before bed should be on the lighter side.

- **Don't do work in bed.** To build a link in your mind between sleeping and being in bed. It's best not to use your bed for work or other activities that stimulate your brain.

Finally, you can also optimize your bedroom to promote tranquility. Again, there is no one-size-fits-all, but here are some tips you can consider in setting your bedroom up for good sleep. You may not have considered these things before, as sleeping in your carefree youth may have been different. Take it from someone older, if not wiser, than you: these small things can make a big difference!

- **Use a comfortable mattress and pillow.** Your sleeping surface is critical to comfort and pain-free sleep, so choose your bedding wisely. The sheets and blankets are the first thing you touch when you get into bed, so make sure they match your needs and preferences.

- **Make your room cool.** Not, like, a cool place for your friends to hang out, but a cool 65 degrees or so (which actually might be so cool that your friends won't want to hang out there — but you'll be sleeping, so you won't mind). Certainly, fine-tune your bedroom temperature to suit your preferences, but err on the cooler side.

- **Block out light.** Use heavy curtains or an eye mask to prevent light from interrupting your sleep.

- **Drown out noise.** Ear plugs can stop noise from keeping you awake, and if you don't find them comfortable, try a white noise machine or even a fan to drown out bothersome sounds.

- **Try calming scents.** As we discussed earlier, aromatherapy is a good relaxation technique. Light smells, such as lavender (which you already know is my favorite) may induce a calmer state of mind and help cultivate a positive space for sleep.

To sum it up, sleep is important. You may not be used to thinking about your sleep, or you may not be used to regulating your sleep and wake-up times. But since sleep is as essential as food and water, it makes sense that you pay attention to it. Proper sleep will allow both your brain and body to function at a more optimal level. Sleep on that!

Stop and Reflect:
Sleep on It

Look at your Sleep Diary and answer these questions:

- Can you identify any patterns, positive or negative, which affected your sleep?

  _____
  _____
  _____
  _____
  _____

- How has being in law school affected your sleep habits?

  _____
  _____
  _____
  _____
  _____

- What three tips can you easily try to incorporate into your daily routine to try to improve your sleep?

  _____
  _____
  _____
  _____
  _____

CHAPTER SEVEN

Nutrition

*Even in this high-tech age, the low-tech plant continues
to be the key to nutrition and health.*

JACK WEATHERFORD

B y now you can probably see and appreciate the interconnectedness of each topic and realize that our brains are affected by most of what we do. You may not have given much thought to your overall diet before. Although food has classically been perceived as a way to provide energy and building material to the body, its ability to prevent and protect against diseases is starting to be recognized. In particular, research over the last five years has provided exciting evidence for the influence of food on specific molecular systems and mechanisms that maintain mental function. Over thousands of years, diet, in conjunction with other aspects of daily living, such as exercise, has come to play a crucial role in shaping cognitive capacity and brain evolution. A poor diet can lead to a host of medical issues like obesity, cardiovascular disease, diabetes, and certain cancers. But diet also influences the brain and can increase the risk for mental disorders and neurodegenerative diseases.

Think about this: every aspect of our lives is controlled by our brains — our thoughts, movements, breathing, heartbeat, senses, and more. And like everything else in our bodies, the brain requires energy — in the form of the foods we eat. Your brain is always "on;" it works hard 24/7, even while you're asleep. This means your brain requires a constant supply of fuel. That "fuel" comes from the foods you eat — and what's in that fuel makes all the difference. In fact, the brain uses 20% of our caloric needs. Put simply, what you eat directly affects the structure and function of your brain, and ultimately, your mood. Your main job in law school is to learn: to use your brain. Therefore, it's incredibly important what you feed it.

What should you feed your brain? Your brain needs special materials to run properly: glucose, vitamins, minerals, and other essential chemicals. For example, the energy for your brain is glucose. You can get glucose by eating carbohydrates or other foods that can be converted to glucose. Your brain must manufacture the right proteins and fats to do things such as grow new connections. You do this by digesting proteins and fats in food and your brain uses the pieces, that is, the amino acids and fatty acids, to make new brain proteins and fats. Without the correct amount and balance of particular building blocks, your brain will not work properly. You may know that a nutritious diet full of whole grains, fruits, vegetables, dairy, nuts, seeds, and protein is good for your health. In contrast, eating processed foods and beverages high in saturated animal fat and sugar — like processed meats, cookies, candy, sugary drinks, and potato chips — can be very harmful to your health. Eating these types of foods regularly can cause diseases such as obesity and diabetes. Because processed foods, sugary drinks, and candy are very easy to find, are cheap, and can be tasty (who doesn't like a candy bar, or a slice of pizza?), it is no surprise that obesity and diabetes are two of the most common diseases in the world.

These nutritional facts are important to your success as a law student and future lawyer because foods high in fat and sugar can do more than make us obese or diabetic — they can also affect our brains. To help set yourself up to perform your best, mentally and physically, don't make your diet an afterthought. Yes, it takes thought and preparation to eat healthy, but that effort will directly benefit you, and even your clients, as you put your brain in its best position to perform.

What is a healthy diet? It need not be overly complicated. The healthier choices you make, ideally the healthier you will be. There is extensive research on the various diets which have become popular, and experts have settled on a plan to *"eat real food, not much, and mostly plants."*[57] For example, a diet based on a variety of minimally processed vegetable, fruits, whole grains, legumes, nuts, and seeds (known as a "whole foods, plant-based" diet) is simple, is easy to follow, and has been shown to prevent and even reverse some health conditions.

Drink water. Lots of it. Even mild dehydration, which can come on after not drinking for a few hours, especially if you are active or working in a warm environment, reduces energy, negatively affects mood, and makes it more difficult to concentrate (I decided that my slight fogginess as I write just might be from mild dehydration, so I took a short break to get a glass of water). If you prefer other beverages than water, that is fine so long as they are not overly sweetened. Just drink.

Tips for Eating Better
(or, an apple a day is a good start)

Here are some of the healthiest brain foods you should try to incorporate into your diet. Now, I understand, you are in law school and it may seem daunting if you are primarily eating at a school cafeteria, rushing to make meals between classes and studying, or grabbing food on the go when there isn't time to cook. But with just a little planning, you can still make healthy choices. Consider packing your lunch, or at least some healthy snacks, so that you don't just reach for the quickest and easiest food when you are hungry. Plus, you'll save money! And don't let these lists intimidate you; remember, it's just as easy to buy a bag of nuts as it is a candy bar at the drug store. Granola, yogurt, air-popped popcorn, and trail mix are all easy-to-find snacks. And, most university cafeterias offer healthy choices, whether it is a salad bar or prepackaged salads and fruits.

Oily fish. Oily fish contains omega-3, which can help boost brain health. Omega-3s help build membranes around each cell in the body, including the brain cells. They can, therefore, improve the structure of brain cells called neurons. Studies have found that people with high levels of omega-3s had increased blood flow in the brain. The researchers also identified a connection between omega-3 levels and better cognition, or thinking abilities.[58] These results suggest that eating foods rich in omega-3s, such as oily fish, may boost brain function.

Examples of oily fish that contain high levels of omega-3s include:

- salmon
- mackerel
- tuna

- herring

- sardines

You can also get omega-3s from soybeans, nuts, flaxseed, and other seeds. A good tip: you can buy prepackaged tuna and salmon at the grocery store, or even places like CVS, Walgreens, and Target. These packages are portable and affordable and can easily be added to a salad or sandwich to make a healthier meal.

Dark chocolate. Dark chocolate contains cocoa, also known as cacao. Cacao contains flavonoids, a type of antioxidant. Antioxidants are especially important for brain health, as the brain is highly susceptible to oxidative stress, which contributes to age-related cognitive decline and brain diseases. Cacao flavonoids seem to be good for the brain, as they may help reverse memory problems. Studies support the brain-boosting effects of dark chocolate. In one such study, researchers used imaging methods to look at activity in the brain after participants ate chocolate with at least 70% cacao. The researchers concluded that eating this type of dark chocolate may improve brain plasticity, which is crucial for learning, and may also provide other brain-related benefits. Any research that supports eating chocolate is good news to me!

Berries. Like dark chocolate, many berries contain flavonoid antioxidants. Research suggests that these may make the berries good food for the brain. Antioxidants help by reducing inflammation and oxidative stress. The antioxidants in berries include anthocyanin, caffeic acid, catechin, and quercetin. The antioxidant compounds in berries have many positive effects on the brain, including:

- improving communication between brain cells

- reducing inflammation throughout the body

- increasing plasticity, which helps brain cells form new connections, boosting learning and memory

- reducing or delaying age-related neurodegenerative diseases and cognitive decline

Antioxidant-rich berries that can boost brain health include:

- strawberries
- blackberries
- blueberries
- black currants
- mulberries

Nuts and seeds. Nuts and seeds are plant-based sources of healthful fats and proteins. Eating more nuts and seeds may be good for the brain, as these foods contain omega-3 fatty acids and antioxidants. Higher overall nut intake has been linked to better brain function in older age. Nuts and seeds are also good sources of the antioxidant vitamin E, which protects cells from oxidative stress caused by free radicals. As a person ages, their brain may be exposed to this form of oxidative stress, and vitamin E may therefore support brain health in older age. Vitamin E may also contribute to improved cognition and reduced risk of Alzheimer's disease. The nuts and seeds with the highest amounts of vitamin E include:

- sunflower seeds
- almonds
- hazelnuts

Whole grains. Eating whole grains is another way to benefit from the effects of vitamin E, with these grains being a good source of the vitamin.

Whole-grain foods include:

- brown rice
- barley

- bulgur wheat
- oatmeal
- whole-grain bread
- whole-grain pasta

Coffee. Coffee is a well-known concentration aid — many drink it to stay awake and encourage focus. The caffeine in coffee blocks a substance in the brain called adenosine, which makes a person feel sleepy. Beyond boosting alertness, studies suggest that caffeine may also increase the brain's capacity for processing information. Researchers have found that caffeine causes an increase in brain entropy, which refers to complex and variable brain activity. When entropy is high, the brain can process more information.

Coffee is also a source of antioxidants, which may support brain health as a person gets older. One study has linked lifelong coffee consumption with reduced risk of:

- cognitive decline
- stroke
- Parkinson's disease
- Alzheimer's disease[59]

Caffeine can, however, affect a person's sleep and doctors do not recommend caffeine consumption for everyone. The amount you can tolerate before it interferes with your sleep can vary as well. Remember caffeine's "half-life," which we learned about in the chapter called Sleep.

Avocados. A source of healthful unsaturated fat, avocados may support the brain. Plus, they are tasty. Who doesn't like a little guacamole? (Watch out for the chips, though.) Eating monounsaturated fats is thought to reduce blood pressure, and high blood pressure is linked with cognitive decline. Thus, by reducing high blood pressure, the unsaturated fats in avocados may lower the risk of cognitive decline.

Other sources of healthful unsaturated fats include:

- almonds, cashews, and peanuts
- flaxseed and chia seeds
- soybean, sunflower, and canola oils
- walnuts and Brazil nuts
- fish

Peanuts. Peanuts are a legume (not a nut!) with an excellent nutritional profile. They contain plenty of unsaturated fats and protein to keep a person's energy levels up throughout the day. Peanuts also provide key vitamins and minerals to keep the brain healthy, including high levels of vitamin E and resveratrol.

Resveratrol is a natural non-flavonoid antioxidant found in peanuts, mulberries, and rhubarb. Evidence suggests that resveratrol can have protective effects, such as helping to prevent cancers, inflammation, and neurological diseases, including Alzheimer's and Parkinson's.

Eggs. Enjoyed by many for breakfast, eggs can be an effective brain food. They are a good source of the following B vitamins:

- vitamin B-6
- vitamin B-12
- folic acid

Recent research suggests that these vitamins may prevent brain shrinkage and delay cognitive decline.

Broccoli. Broccoli and other cruciferous vegetables are rich in fiber and nutrients. As well as being a low-calorie source of dietary fiber, broccoli may be good for the brain. It is rich in compounds called glucosinolates. When the body breaks these down, they produce isothiocyanates. Isothiocyanates are thought to reduce oxidative stress and lower the risk of neurodegenerative diseases. Broccoli also contains Vitamin C and flavonoids, and these antioxidants can further boost a person's brain health. Other cruciferous vegetables that contain glucosinolates include:

- brussels sprouts
- bok choy
- cabbage
- cauliflower
- turnips
- kale

Kale. Leafy greens, including kale, may support brain health. Like broccoli, kale contains glucosinolates, and leafy greens also contain other key antioxidants, vitamins, and minerals. This is why many consider kale to be a superfood.

Soy Products. Soybean products are rich in a particular group of antioxidants called polyphenols. Research links polyphenols with a reduced risk of dementia and improved cognitive abilities in regular aging processes. Soy products contain polyphenols called isoflavones, including daidzein and genistein. These chemicals act as antioxidants, providing a range of health benefits throughout the body.

*

The foods listed above may help improve your memory and concentration. Some may also reduce the risk of stroke and age-related neurodegenerative diseases, such as Alzheimer's and Parkinson's. Some of the foods contain compounds such as healthful fatty acids, which can help improve the structure of neurons. Other compounds, such as sugars and saturated fats, may damage brain cell structures.

In sum, brain-boosting foods tend to contain one or more of the following:

- antioxidants, such as flavonoids or vitamin E
- B vitamins
- healthful fats
- omega-3 fatty acids

Foods to Avoid

(well, mostly avoid; I like doughnuts too)

Of course, there are certain foods it is best to avoid (or at least, not overly indulge in; I would never suggest you completely avoid something you love). We all enjoy a treat now and then or have a favorite food that may not be the healthiest choice. I would never tell you to avoid those foods altogether; that won't be sustainable in the long run. That's why I have never been a fan of fad diets or cleanses that promise amazing results quickly. That behavior is not sustainable and often leads to overindulgence once the diet or cleanse is over. Remember that healthy eating should be a way of life, not a diet. So, with that in mind, here are some foods to minimize consumption of.

Refined sugars. Sugar is one of the best examples of refined carbohydrates. Other examples include highly processed grains such as flour. The glycemic index (GI) of these refined carbs is high. These carbs are easily digested by the body and can increase your blood sugar and insulin levels. Having excessive quantities of foods with high GI has been often linked with damaging the functioning of the brain. Healthier alternatives include legumes, whole grains, vegetables, and fruits.

Alcohol. The negative effects of alcohol on the body are endless. Excessive consumption can have a serious impact on your brain as well. Regular consumption of alcohol can cause metabolic changes in the body and also disrupt the functioning of neurotransmitters — the chemicals used by the brain for the purpose of communication. Also, people who are addicted to alcohol can develop a deficiency of vitamin B1. This deficiency can increase risks of brain disorders.

It is important to note that substance abuse is a problem for lawyers. While a drink or two from time to time is certainly not unhealthy, be wary of using those drinks to "relax" or "unwind." If you drink alcohol or use drugs as a coping mechanism, that will only lead to bigger problems. In fact, at least 25% of attorneys who face formal disciplinary charges from their state bar are identified as suffering from addiction or other mental illness, with substance abuse playing at least some role in 60% of all disciplinary cases. Furthermore, approximately 60% of all malpractice claims and 85% of all trust fund violation cases involve substance abuse.[60]

Instead, try to relax or unwind using the healthy suggestions we have discussed in this book. If you find that you may be overconsuming, or you are worried about a friend, get help. The ABA Directory of Lawyer Assistance Programs is a good place to start: https://www.americanbar.org/groups/lawyer_assistance/resources/lap_programs_by_state/.

Sugary drinks. Sugary drinks like energy drinks, fruit juices and sodas can be harmful for your brain. Not only do these drinks contribute to weight gain, they can increase risks like Alzheimer's disease and dementia. Maybe you're not worried about Alzheimer's quite yet — I know, I've got a few years on you. But sugar also causes brain fog — that feeling of being unable to focus or feeling groggy. And I think we can agree that groggy isn't good for studying. Try water flavored with lime, lemon, cucumber, mint, strawberries, or other fruit instead.

Highly processed foods. Highly processed foods are also high in salt, fats, and sugar. Foods like instant noodles, chips, ready-made meals, and sauces bought from stores all come under the category of highly processed foods. Not only are these foods high in calories, but they are low in nutrient content as well. Heavily processed foods can cause inflammation in the brain, slowing your thought process and impairing memory.

Fresh sources of foods are the best alternatives to these highly processed foods. Fresh fruits, vegetables, nuts, legumes, fish, and meat are all healthy foods which can have a positive impact on your brain.

Foods with high quantities of trans fats. Trans fats come under the category of unsaturated fats, which can be harmful for brain health. Even more harmful are the artificial trans fats, which can be found in packaged foods, prepackaged biscuits, and ready-made cakes, to name a very few. These are harmful to your heart as well.

As an alternative, try foods with unsaturated fats like chia seeds, walnuts, flaxseed, and fish, all of which can be good for your brain. Make your own trail mix with healthy nuts and seeds and carry it with you to avoid trips to the vending machine. Among my favorite home-made snacks are protein balls, made with oats, peanut butter, flaxseed, maple syrup or honey, protein powder, and coconut. Simple, easy, satisfying, and so much healthier than grabbing a candy bar or chips.

*

The USDA has helpful online tools to help. In particular, My-Plate Plan[61] on the USDA website can help you determine your overall caloric needs and recommended daily amounts of different types of food. The USDA's tips for creating a healthy meal are contained in the Appendix.

Maybe you find all this information on nutrition overwhelming. Perhaps you've never given your overall diet much thought. I know it may seem daunting to plan your meals if you haven't done so before, especially when you are busy with classes and all that law school entails. Start with small steps that are easily maintained. It's truly about changing your behavior patterns, rather than making individual changes. By slowly creating a lifestyle that supports health, you'll escape the need to rely on willpower, which is a finite resource, and be successful because your entire day will be organized around the habits that make you the best version of yourself. Your brain and body will thank you!

Stop and Reflect:
You Are What You Eat

1. Look at the list of healthy foods and list the ones you have eaten today.

   I haven't eaten much today besides
   donut and coffee

2. Now list the foods you have eaten today which you should avoid.

   Donut - not common, rare treat

3. Reflect on your lists and plan how you can improve what you eat tomorrow.

   I can eat more veggies and
   proteins

Stop and Reflect on
Your Reflections

(or, let's not call it a day quite yet)

N ow that you have read the whole book and completed the end-of-chapter reflections, let's take a few moments for a final self-reflection. Self-reflection can help you take the material in this book and consciously begin implementing its suggestions into your life.

Put your phone and laptop in another room. Set a timer, tomato or other, for 25 minutes. Sit with just this book and a pencil and paper, look over your "Stop and Reflect" answers from each chapter or section, listed below for your convenience, and answer the following questions.

➲ What three things from this chapter can I implement today?

➲ What three things can I implement this week?

➲ What three things can I implement this month?

➲ What final thoughts do I have after reading the book and completing all the reflections?

Conclusion

(or, this is not the end, friend)

nitially, I struggled as I tried to write this conclusion. It dawned on me that I was struggling because I called it a "conclusion." When it comes to brain health and wellness, there is no "conclusion." The path is circular, continuous, and evolving. You may be challenged in various areas as you navigate the rest of law school and transition to practice. Remember that your brain is the asset on which clients will rely, and therefore, you should work to strengthen it and promote its health. By working now to understand how to care for your brain, body, and your overall wellbeing, you will have the knowledge and skills to meet the challenges ahead. Remember, you've only got one brain. Do everything you can to take care of it. Your brain, your body — and eventually, your clients — will thank you.

Appendix

Here is a four-step mindful studying process you can use to help foster focus when you study.

Set your intention. Set your intention before you begin your study session. Avoid just opening a book and beginning to read. Make your goals concrete, and not simply time guidelines, e.g., "I will read three Property cases and answer a hypothetical," not "I will work on Property for two hours." By consciously deciding what you want to accomplish, you will have a greater chance of accomplishing it. It won't just be a happy coincidence or a failed study session.

Clear your physical space. Choose a physical space that is conducive to your work. Have all the materials and space needed to do your work. Put your smartphone away (not just face down). Turn off any automatic alerts. Know that each time you start and stop studying, you leak a little mental efficiency. In fact, one study revealed that pot smokers were more efficient than multitaskers. Knowing that should motivate you not to multitask.

Continued

Continued

Clear your mental space. Purposeful breathing for a few minutes is an easy and simple way to clear your mind. Close your eyes, put both feet on the ground, open your palms face up in your lap, and breathe deeply, in through the nose and out through the mouth. Just two minutes of focused breathing will calm your nervous system and helps to clear away distracting thoughts.

Ready, set, work. Now that you've set your intention and cleared your physical and mental space, you are ready to work. Jot down thoughts which intrude so you can attend to them later. Try not to get caught up thinking about grades or other issues, and refocus your attention on the work at hand.

Running Meditation

Before you start running, inhale deeply. Hold your breath for a few seconds, and exhale. Do this for a few minutes or so, and you will experience a deep relaxation before your run. If you find the waiting too difficult, try to start with one minute of stillness—or as much as you can stand—and work up to more minutes.

Set an intention. It could be a question that has been haunting you for days, or a stressful thought or challenge that has been on your mind. You don't have to know what the resolution might be—just put faith out there that this walk or run will help it.

Choose a mantra. Choose some words that mean something to you, like "I am strong," and keep repeating them as you walk or run. This anchors your attention and keeps you in the present moment. Tether the mantra to your footfalls, so you are using one word per footfall.

Focus on your breath and posture. You can count your breaths and picture your back straight and lungs filling with air. You should feel energized by this focus.

Take in your surroundings. If you are running outside, keenly observe nature and feel the wind, the sun, the air.

Thank yourself for making the effort. And as you run or walk, note the thoughts that cross your mind, acknowledge them, and go back to your mantra or breath counting or whatever focus works for you.

Walking Meditation

Before you start walking, inhale deeply. Hold your breath for a few seconds, and exhale. Do this for a few minutes or so, and you will experience a deep relaxation before your walk. If you find the waiting too difficult, try to start with one minute of stillness — or as much as you can stand — and work up to more minutes.

Follow your own footsteps. As you begin walking, deliberately put your mind down into your feet. Become aware of the physical movement of your legs. Notice the sensations of the contact of your feet on the ground. Be interested in the quality of each step. Are your legs tense or relaxed?

Switch on your senses. Stay connected to the physicality of your legs and feet, and expand your awareness to notice your surroundings. Notice the people passing by, the buildings, the color of the doorways; look up and check out the sky...be curious. Actively listen. Tune into the sounds around you, especially if you like them: birdsong, someone's cheery whistling, kind words overheard, or perhaps even silence. If you don't notice anything pleasant, play one of your favorite songs in your head and listen to that.

Guard your inner peace. We experience the world and ourselves through our senses. By paying friendly attention to the relay of information we're receiving through them every second, the happier and more connected to our surroundings we become. Think of your mind as your home. Instead of letting any old stranger barge into your sanctuary and potentially upset the balance, in being mindful you stand at the front door, check out who's there, and then decide who comes in. With practice, you can become expert at only allowing health and happiness-restoring thoughts.

Look for the good. Left to its own devices, your mind can get negative: "It's cold!' or "What is that kid doing?" But you have a choice. Get stressed by your stress, or switch tracks and choose to have thoughts that boost your wellbeing. All you need to do is look for the positives during your walk. The blue sky, fresh air on your face, a child's laugh, someone's beautiful smile. It could even be a stylish pair of shoes. Keeping an eye out for beauty is way more relaxing than staying caught in the hamster wheel of negativity. This simple switch in attitude can have a profound impact on your day.

Sample Weekly Productivity Journal

Five most important tasks of the week:

1. _____
2. _____
3. _____
4. _____
5. _____

Other things I'd like to get done:

1. _____
2. _____
3. _____
4. _____
5. _____

Additional tasks:

1. _____
2. _____
3. _____
4. _____
5. _____

Exercise plan for the week:

_____

_____

_____

_____

_____

_____

_____

Meal plan for the week:

_____

_____

_____

_____

_____

_____

_____

Sample Daily Productivity Journal

Get Things Done!

My day:

7:00 _____

8:00 _____

9:00 _____

10:00 _____

11:00 _____

12:00 _____

1:00 _____

2:00 _____

3:00 _____

4:00 _____

5:00 _____

6:00 _____

7:00 _____

8:00 _____

9:00 _____

Tomorrow I need to do this:

1. _____

2. _____

3. _____

Today's focus:

_____

_____

_____

Today's to-do list:

_____

_____

_____

_____

Exercise: _____

_____

Breakfast:_____

Lunch: _____

Dinner: _____

Today I am grateful for:

1. _____

2. _____

3. _____

Wellness Tracker

Week of:

	MONDAY	TUESDAY	WEDNESDAY
SLEEP			
WATER			
EXERCISE			
VITAMINS			
MEALS			
MOOD			
ENERGY			

THURSDAY	FRIDAY	SATURDAY	SUNDAY

APPENDIX

Nine Tips to Build a Healthy Meal

1. Make half your plate veggies and fruits.

Vegetables and fruits are full of nutrients that support good health. Choose fruits and red, orange, and dark-green vegetables such as tomatoes, sweet potatoes, and broccoli.

2. Include whole grains.

Aim to make at least half your grains whole grains. Look for the words "100% whole grain" or "100% whole wheat" on the food label. Whole grains provide more nutrients, like fiber, than refined grains.

3. Don't forget the dairy.

Complete your meal with a cup of fat-free or low-fat milk. You will get the same amount of calcium and other essential nutrients as whole milk but fewer calories. Don't drink milk? Try a soy beverage (soy milk) as your drink or include low-fat yogurt in your meal or snack.

4. Add lean protein.

Choose protein foods such as lean beef, pork, chicken, or turkey, and eggs, nuts, beans, or tofu. Twice a week, make seafood the protein on your plate.

5. Avoid extra fat.

Using heavy gravies or sauces will add fat and calories to otherwise healthy choices. Try steamed broccoli with a sprinkling of low-fat Parmesan cheese or a squeeze of lemon.

6. Get creative in the kitchen.

Whether you are making a sandwich, a stir-fry, or a casserole, find ways to make them healthier. Try using less meat and cheese, which can be higher in saturated fat and sodium, and adding in more veggies that add new flavors and textures to your meals.

7. Take control of your food.

Eat at home more often so you know exactly what you are eating. If you eat out, check and compare the nutrition information of different dishes. Choose options that are lower in calories, saturated fat, and sodium.

8. Try new foods.

Keep it interesting by picking out new foods you've never tried before, like mango, lentils, quinoa, kale, or sardines. You may find a new favorite! Trade fun and tasty recipes with friends or find them online.

9. Satisfy your sweet tooth in a healthy way.

Indulge in a naturally sweet dessert dish — fruit! Serve a fresh fruit salad or a fruit parfait made with yogurt. For a hot dessert, bake apples and top with cinnamon.

Additional Resources

Books

David Allen, *Making It All Work* (2008).

Jeena Cho and Karen Gifford, *The Anxious Lawyer: An 8-Week Guide to a Joyful and Satisfying Law Practice Through Mindfulness and Meditation* (2016).

Mihaly Csikszentmihalyi, *Flow: The Psychology of Optimal Experience* (2008).

Richard Davidson, *The Emotional Life of Your Brain* (2012).

Carol S. Dweck, *Mindset: The New Psychology of Success* (2006).

Angela Duckworth, *Grit* (2016).

Beth Frates, et al., *Lifestyle Medicine Handbook: An Introduction to the Power of Healthy Habits* (2019).

Winifred Gallagher, *Rapt Attention and the Focused Life* (2009).

Shailini George, et al., *Mindful Lawyering: The Key to Creative Problem Solving* (2018).

Daniel Gilbert, *Stumbling on Happiness* (2007).

Edward M. Hallowell, *Driven to Distraction at Work* (2015).

Thich Nhat Hanh, *The Miracle of Mindfulness* (1975).

Thich Nhat Hanh, *You Are Here* (2001).

Lawrence Krieger, *The Hidden Sources of Law School Stress: Avoiding Mistakes That Create Unhappy and Unprofessional Lawyers* (2014).

Nancy Levit and Douglas O. Linder, *The Happy Lawyer: Making a Good Life in the Law* (2010).

Kelly McGonigle, *The Willpower Instinct: How Self Control Works, Why it Matters, and What You Can Do to Get More of It* (2012).

Cal Newport, *Deep Work: Rules for Focused Success in a Distracted World* (2016).

Scott Rogers, *Mindfulness for Law Students* (2009).

Scott Rogers, *The Six Minute Solution: A Mindfulness Primer for Lawyers* (2009).

Susan Smalley, *Fully Present: The Science, Art, and Practice of Mindfulness* (2010).

Alex Soojung-Kim Pang, *Rest* (2016).

Kathryne Young, *How to Be Sort of Happy in Law School* (2018).

Articles

Cheryl Krause and Jane Chong, *Lawyer Wellbeing as a Crisis of the Profession*, (July 1, 2019). South Carolina Law Review, forthcoming, available at SSRN: https://ssrn.com/abstract=3464992.

Sophie Leroy, *Why Is It So Hard to Do My Work? The Challenge of Attention Residue When Switching Between Work Tasks*, Organizations Behavior and Human Decision Processes 109 (2009).

Lawrence Krieger, *Institutional Denial about the Dark Side of Law School, and Fresh Empirical Guidance for Constructively Breaking the Silence*, 52 J. Legal Educ. 112, 117 (2002).

Lawrence Krieger and Kennon Sheldon, *What Makes Lawyers Happy? A Data-Driven Prescription to Redefine Professional Success*, 83 George Wash. L. Rev. 544 (2015).

Jarrod Reich, *Capitalizing on Healthy Lawyers: The Business Case for Law Firms to Promote and Prioritize Lawyer Well-Being*, 65 Villanova L. Rev. 361 (2020).

Christine Rosen, *The Myth of Multitasking*, 20 New Atlantis 105 (2008).

Charity Scott, *Mindfulness in Law: A Path to Well-Being and Balance for Lawyers and Law Students*, 60 Ariz. L. Rev. 635 (2018).

Magazines

Time Magazine, *Special Edition: The Science of Happiness: New Discoveries for a More Joyful Life* (September 20, 2019).

Time Magazine, *Special Edition: Wellness: Finding a Happier You* (May 7, 2019).

Time Magazine, *Special Edition: Mindfulness: The New Science of Health and Happiness* (April 7, 2017).

Online Resources

AmericanBar.org, *Resources for Law Students and Law Schools*, available at https://www.americanbar.org/groups/lawyer_ assistance/articles_and_info/law_student_resources/#podcasts.

AmericanBar.org, *Wellbeing Toolkit for Lawyers and Legal Employers*, available at https://www.americanbar.org/content/dam/aba/ administrative/lawyer_assistance/ls_colap_wellbeing_toolkit_ for_lawyers_legal_employers.authcheckdam.pdf.

Nicholas Carr, *Is Google Making Us Stupid?* The Atlantic (July/August 2008) available at https://www.theatlantic.com/magazine/ archive/2008/07/is-google-making-us-stupid/306868/.

Massachusetts Supreme Judicial Court Steering Committee on Lawyer Wellbeing Report to the Justices, July 15, 2019, available at https://www.mass.gov/doc/supreme-judicial-court-steering-committee-on-lawyer-well-being-report-to-the-justices/ download.

Alice Park, *The Power of Sleep*, Time.com, September 11, 2014, available at https://time.com/3326565/the-power-of-sleep/.

Podcast

Vedantam, Shankar, Hidden Brain, *You 2.0: The Value Of 'Deep Work' In an Age of Distraction*, https://www.npr.org/2017/07/25/539092670/you-2-0-the-value-of-deep-work-in-an-age-of-distraction.

Apps

Calm

Evernote

Headspace

Insight Timer

10% Happier

Todoist

Endnotes

Chapter One: The Wellbeing Crisis

1. Patrick Krill, et al., *The Prevalence of Substance Abuse and Other Mental Health Concerns Among American Attorneys*, 10 J. Addiction Med., 46 (2016); ABA press coverage regarding the landmark study and other resources can be found here: https://abacolap.wordpress.com/2016/02/08/new-study-from-aba-and-hazelden-released-gets-widespread-coverage/ and here: https://thebarexaminer.org/article/bar-admissions/the-report-of-the-national-task-force-on-lawyer-well-being-and-the-role-of-the-bar-admissions-community-in-the-lawyer-well-being-movement/.

2. National Task Force on Lawyer Wellbeing, *The Path to Lawyer Wellbeing: Practical Recommendations for Positive Change* (2017), cover letter by Task Force co-chairs Bree Buchanan, Esq., Director, Texas Lawyers Assistance Program, State Bar of Texas, and James C. Coyle, Esq., Attorney Regulation Counsel, Colorado Supreme Court.

3. *Massachusetts Supreme Judicial Court Steering Committee on Lawyer Wellbeing Report to the Justices,* July 15, 2019, available at https://www.mass.gov/doc/supreme-judicial-court-steering-committee-on-lawyer-well-being-report-to-the-justices/download.

4. National Task Force on Lawyer Wellbeing, *The Path to Lawyer Wellbeing: Practical Recommendations for Positive Change* (2017), https://lawyerwellbeing.net/the-report.

5. Lawrence S. Krieger, *Institutional Denial about the Dark Side of Law School, and Fresh Empirical Guidance for Constructively Breaking the Silence*, 52 J. Legal Educ. 112, 117 (2002).

6. Imposter Syndrome? 8 Tactics to Combat the Anxiety: https://www.americanbar.org/news/abanews/publications/youraba/2018/october-2018/tell-yourself-_yet--and-other-tips-for-overcoming-impostor-syndr/.

7. Martin E.P. Seligman, *Authentic Happiness* 177 (2002); *see also* Martin E.P. Seligman, Paul R. Verkuil & Terry H. Kang, *Why Lawyers are Unhappy*, 23 Cardozo L. Rev. 33 (2001).

8. https://lawyerwellbeing.net/the-report.

9. Centers for Disease Control and Prevention: Healthy Aging, What Is a Healthy Brain? New Research Explores Perceptions of Cognitive Health Among Diverse Older Adults, which can be found at: https://www.cdc.gov/aging/pdf/perceptions_of_cog_hlth_factsheet.pdf.

Chapter Two: Cultivating Focus in the 24/7 Digital Age

10. *Parietal Lobe*, Sciencedirect.com, available at http://www.sciencedirect.com/topics/neuroscience/parietal-lobe.

11. Amy Arnsten, *Stress Signaling Pathways That Impair Prefrontal Cortex Structure and Function*, 10 Nat. Rev. Neuroscience 410–422 (2009), also available at https://www.ncbi.nlm.nih.gov/pmc/articles/PMC2907136/.

12. Cal Newport, *Deep Work: Rules for Focused Success in a Distracted World* 84 (2016).

13. *Deep Work*, p. 40.

14. John Tierney, *When the Mind Wanders, Happiness Also Strays*, N.Y. Times, Nov. 15, 2010, available at: https://www.nytimes.com/2010/11/16/science/16tier.html.

15. Vanessa Loder, *Why Multitasking Is Worse Than Marijuana for Your IQ*, Forbes, June 11, 2014, available at https://www.forbes.com/sites/vanessaloder/2014/06/11/why-multi-tasking-is-worse-than-marijuana-for-your-iq/?sh=42a376707c11.

16. Adrian F. Ward, Kristen Duke, Ayelet Gneezy, Maarten W. Bos, *Brain Drain: The Mere Presence of One's Own Smartphone Reduces Available Cognitive Capacity*, J. of the Assoc. for Consumer Res. 2 (2) (2017).

17. *Tibetan Monks Can Change Their Metabolism*, Mind Matters News, September 19, 2109, available at https://mindmatters.ai/2019/09/tibetan-monks-can-change-their-metabolism/

18. Joanne Gray, *Solve Problems by Tapping into Your Unconscious Mind*, Financial Review, July 10, 2015, available at https://www.afr.com/work-and-careers/management/solve-problems-by-tapping-into-your-unconscious-mind-20150621-ghtf0z.

19. Tim Kreider, *The 'Busy' Trap*, N.Y. Times, June 30, 2012, available at https://opinionator.blogs.nytimes.com/2012/06/30/the-busy-trap/.

20. *Deep Work*, p. 155.

21. *Deep Work*, p. 157.

22. Jonathon Webb, *Do People Choose Pain Over Boredom?* BBC News Online, July 14, 2014, available at https://www.bbc.com/news/science-environment-28130690.

23. Jeffrey James, *How Steve Jobs Trained His Own Brain*, Inc.com, March 19, 2015, available at https://www.inc.com/geoffrey-james/how-steve-jobs-trained-his-own-brain.html.

24. Shailini Jandial George, *The Cure for the Distracted Mind: Why Law Schools Should Teach Mindfulness*, 53 Duq. L. Rev. (Winter 2015).

25. Steve Bradt, *Wandering Mind Is Not a Happy Mind*, The Harvard Gazette, November 11, 2020, available at https://news.harvard.edu/gazette/story/2010/11/wandering-mind-not-a-happy-mind/.

26. Lynette L. Craft and Frank M. Perna, *The Benefits of Exercise for the Clinically Depressed*, J. Clin. Psychiatry, 6 (3) 104–111 (2004), available at https://www.ncbi.nlm.nih.gov/pmc/articles/PMC474733/.

27. Just to name a few: Haruki Murakami, *What I Talk About When I Am Running* (2007); Jen A. Miller, *Running: A Love Story* (2016); Caleb Daniloff, *Running Ransom Road* (2013).

28. *Why Remote Working Will Be the New Normal Even after COVID-19*, EY.com, April 8, 2020, available at https://www.ey.com/en_be/covid-19/why-remote-working-will-be-the-new-normal-even-after-covid-19.

29. Tim Herrera, *Don't Work on Your Party Laptop or Party on Your Work Laptop*, N.Y. Times, October 23, 2020, available at https://www.nytimes.com/2020/10/23/smarter-living/what-not-to-do-work-computer.html?searchResultPosition=3.

30. *New Yorker Fires Staff Writer Jeffrey Toobin after Zoom Exposure Incident*, cbs.com, November 12, 2020, available at https://www.cbsnews.com/news/jeffrey-toobin-fired-by-new-yorker-after-Zoom-call-exposure/.

31. *Kids Interrupt Dad's Live TV Interview*, cnn.com, available at https://www.cnn.com/videos/world/2017/03/10/interview-interrupted-children-newday.cnn.

32. Jena Lee, *A Neuropsychological Exploration of Zoom Fatigue*, Psychiatric Times, November 17, 2020, available at https://www.psychiatrictimes.com/view/psychological-exploration-Zoom-fatigue.

33. Shailini Jandial George, *Teaching the Smartphone Generation: How Cognitive Science Can Improve Learning in Law School*, 66 Me. L. Rev. (Winter 2013), available at https://digitalcommons.mainelaw.maine.edu/cgi/viewcontent.cgi?article=1100&context=mlr.

Chapter Three: Stress

34. Rachel Casper, *The Full Weight of Law School Stress on Law Students Is Different*, Lawyer Well-Being & Mental Health: Massachusetts LAP Blog, January 18, 2019, available at https://www.lclma.org/2019/01/18/the-full-weight-of-law-school-stress-on-law-students-is-different/.

35. *How to Survive Law School Without Losing Your Mind: Impostor Syndrome*, University of Illinois Law Library, last updated October 15, 2020, available at https://libguides.law.illinois.edu/HowtoSurviveLawSchool.

36. *Surviving Tough Times by Building Resilience*, helpguide.com, available at https://www.helpguide.org/articles/stress/surviving-tough-times.htm.

37. *Drowsy Driving vs. Drunk Driving: How Similar Are They?* Sleepfoundation. org, available at https://www.sleepfoundation.org/articles/drowsy-driving-vs-drunk-driving-how-similar-are-they.

38. Casper, *supra* n. 324.

39. Micelle Castillo, *Even a Fake Grin May Help Lower Heart Rate in Stressful Situations*, cbs.com, July 21, 2012, available at https://www.cbsnews.com/news/even-a-fake-grin-may-help-lower-heart-rate-in-stressful-situations/.

Chapter Four: Resilience

40. Mandy Oaklander, *The Science of Bouncing Back*, Time Magazine, May 21, 2015, available at https://time.com/3892044/the-science-of-bouncing-back/.

41. Richard Davidson, *The Emotional Life of Your Brain* (2012).

42. Navy Special Warefare Command, *SEAL Ethos*, available at https://www.nsw.navy.mil/NSW/SEAL-Ethos/.

43. J.S. House, K.R. Landis & D. Umberson, *Social Relationships and Health*, Science Vol. 241 (4865) 540-45 (1988), available at https://science.sciencemag.org/content/241/4865/540.

44. Juliane Holt-Lunstad, Timothy B. Smith & J. Bradley Layton, *Social Relationships and Mortality Risk: A Meta-analytic Review*, PLoS Medicine, available at https://journals.plos.org/plosmedicine/article?id=10.1371/journal.pmed.1000316.

45. American Bar Association, *Directory of Lawyer Assistance Programs*, available at https://www.americanbar.org/groups/lawyer_assistance/resources/lap_programs_by_state/.

46. American Bar Association, *Substance Use and Mental Health Toolkit for Law School Students and Those Who Care about Them*, available at https://docs.google.com/document/d/1Q-2gorCHI4HhwBzihKJI4KR79d0e-AdHicUuX5xX-KTo/edit#.

Chapter Five: Exercise

47. Michelle Ploughman, *Exercise Is Brain Food: The Effects of Physical Activity on Cognitive Function*, J. Developmental Neurorehabilitation, Vol. 11 (3) 236-40 (2008), available at https://pubmed.ncbi.nlm.nih.gov/18781504/.

48. Juliette Tocino-Smith, *10 Neurological Benefits of Exercise*, positivepsychology.com, October 31, 2020, available at https://positivepsychology.com/exercise-neurological-benefits/.

49. Wendy Suzuki, *The Brain-Changing Effects of Exercise*, March 21, 2018, available at https://www.youtube.com/watch?v=BHY0FxzoKZE&list=RDLdDnPYr6R0o&index=8.

50. *Massachusetts Supreme Judicial Court Steering Committee on Lawyer Wellbeing Report to the Justices*, July 15, 2019, available at https://www.mass.gov/doc/supreme-judicial-court-steering-committee-on-lawyer-well-being-report-to-the-justices/download.

51. Lawrence Robinson, Robert Segal & Melinda Smith, *Best Exercises for Health and Weight Loss*, helpguide.com, available at https://www.helpguide.org/articles/healthy-living/what-are-the-best-exercises-for-me.htm.

Chapter Six: Sleep

52. National Institute of Neurological Disorders and Stroke, *Brain Basics: Understanding Sleep*, available at https://www.ninds.nih.gov/Disorders/Patient-Caregiver-Education/Understanding-Sleep.

53. Amy Paturel, *The Benefits of Sleep for Brain Health*, brainandlife.org, February/March 2014, available at https://www.brainandlife.org/articles/could-getting-more-high-quality-sleep-protect-the-brain/.

54. Beth Frates, et al., *Lifestyle Medicine Handbook: An Introduction to the Power of Healthy Habits*, p. 252 (2019).

55. Shahrad Taheri, et al., *Short Sleep Duration Is Associated with Reduced Leptin, Elevated Ghrelin, and Increased Body Mass Index*, PLoS Medicine, available at https://www.ncbi.nlm.nih.gov/pmc/articles/PMC535701/.

Chapter Seven: Nutrition

56. Kristeen Cherney, *How Long Does Caffeine Stay in Your System*, Healthline.com, November 6, 2018, available at https://www.healthline.com/health/how-long-does-caffeine-last.

57. Daniel J. DeNoon, *7 Rules for Eating*, Webmd.com, available at https://www.webmd.com/food-recipes/news/20090323/7-rules-for-eating#1.

58. Lana Burgess, *12 Foods to Boost Brain Function*, medicalnewstoday.com, January 2, 2020, available at https://www.medicalnewstoday.com/articles/324044.

59. Astrid Nehlig, *Effects of Coffee/Caffeine on Brain Health and Disease: What Should I Tell My Patients?* Practical Neurology (April 2016), available at https://pubmed.ncbi.nlm.nih.gov/26677204/.

60. American Bar Association, *If There Is One Bar a Lawyer Cannot Seem to Pass: Alcoholism in the Legal Profession*, available at https://www.americanbar.org/groups/tort_trial_insurance_practice/publications/the_brief/2014-2015/if-there-is-one-bar-a-lawyer-cannot-seem-to-pass--alcoholism-in-/.

61. United States Department of Agriculture, *Get Your My Plate Plan*, USDA.com, available at https://www.choosemyplate.gov/resources/MyPlatePlan.

Index

muscle, 14, 17, 20, 22, 25, 32, 50, 51, 73, 82, 83
music, 31, 35, 60, 93

N
nap, 55, 90, 93
National Suicide Prevention Hotline, 75
National Task Force on Lawyer Wellbeing, 4, 135
Navy SEALs, 66
neurogenesis, 79
neuroplasticity, 79
neuroscientific, 79
neurotransmitters, 79, 109
Newport, Cal, 18, 30, 132, 136
nutrition, viii, 7, 52, 56, 96, 99, 111, 114, 129, 139
nuts, 100–104, 106, 110, 128

O
office of student services, 74
oily fish, 102
Omega-3, 102, 104, 108
oxidative stress, 103, 104, 107

P
parietal lobe, 15, 16, 19, 136
peanuts, 106
perfectionist, 60, 84
pessimism, 5
physiology, 15, 79, 80
plant-based diet, 10, 11, 101
pomodoro, 27, 28
Pomodoro Technique, 27
positive affirmation, 60
power walk, 85
prefrontal cortex, 15, 19, 23, 51, 66, 80
procrastination, 20–22, 24

R
refined sugars, 108
relaxation, 29, 32, 54, 58, 59, 93, 94, 96, 119, 120
resilience, viii, xvi, 25, 54, 57, 62, 65–67, 72, 73, 114, 137, 138
resistance training, 83
resveratrol, 106

S
schedule, vii, 24–28, 30, 44, 54–56, 58, 61, 62, 81, 83, 85, 92, 93
seeds, 100, 101, 103, 104, 106, 110
self-awareness, 70
self-care, 70
self-compassion, 70
shallow work, 19
skiing, 82
skipping rope, 82
sleep, viii, xvi, 7, 10, 11, 25, 50–52, 55, 74, 78, 87–97, 105, 114, 126, 133, 134, 139
sleep deprivation, 55, 89
sleep diary, 89, 90, 97, 114
sleep schedule, 55, 92
social connections, xiv, 10, 11, 55, 67, 69, 81
social media, 13, 18, 23, 27
social support, 56
soy, 107, 128
spiritual, 6, 7, 59, 69, 71
stress, viii, xiv, xvi, 3–6, 10, 11, 33, 46, 49–56, 58–63, 65, 66, 74, 77–79, 82, 83, 89, 91, 93, 103, 104, 107, 114, 121, 132, 136, 137
substance abuse, 74, 89, 109, 135
sugary drinks, 100, 109
swimming, 82, 84

T
tai chi, 82
Task Force Report, 4, 5, 7, 8
trans fat, 110

V
vegetables, 100, 106–108, 110, 128
Vitamin B-12, 106
Vitamin B-6, 106
Vitamin E, 104, 106, 108
vitamins, 100, 106–108, 126

W
walk, 13, 23, 27, 29, 33, 42, 56, 59, 69, 80, 81, 85, 119–121

water, 16, 35, 87, 96, 101, 109, 126, 134
weight training, 81–83, 85
wellbeing, vii, xiv, xv, 3–8, 10, 14, 67, 70, 74, 77, 87, 114, 115, 121, 132, 133, 135, 138
wellbeing crisis, vii, xv, 3, 114, 135
whole grains, 100, 101, 104, 108, 128
working memory, 15, 16, 33, 51

Y
yoga, 56, 58, 59, 70, 82, 83